THE PICTORIAL HISTORY
OF
HOCKEY

THE PICTORIAL HISTORY
— OF —
HOCKEY

JOSEPH ROMAIN

THUNDER BAY
P·R·E·S·S

San Diego, California

Thunder Bay Press
An imprint of the Advantage Publishers Group
5880 Oberlin Drive, San Diego, CA 92121-4794
www.thunderbaybooks.com

All notations of errors or omissions should be addressed to Thunder Bay
Press, editorial department, at the above address. All other correspondence
(author inquiries, permissions) concerning the content of this book should be
addressed to World Publications Group, Inc., 455 Somerset Avenue, North
Dighton, MA 02764, www.wrldpub.com.

ISBN 1-57145-839-5

Library of Congress Cataloging-in Publication Data available upon request.

Printed in China

1 2 3 4 5   06 05 04 03 02

PHOTO CREDITS

Bruce Bennett Studios: J Baker: 241(top); B Bennett: pages 2(inset left),
3(inset left), 6, 8(top right), 114-115, 123, 126, 127, 132, 134, 135, 136, 137,
149, 150-151, 152(both), 153, 154-55, 156, 158, 162(top), 163(both), 164,
165(both), 166(both), 167, 168, 169(both), 170, 171, 172-173(both), 175,
177, 179, 181, 182-183(both), 185(both), 186(both), 187, 189, 190, 191,
192-193(both), 194(both), 195, 196, 197(both), 198, 199(both), 210(top),
202(top), 204, 206(both), 207, 208(both), 209(bottom), 210(both), 212,
214, 214-215, 216, 20(top), 222(bottom), 223, 224, 225, 227(both), 229
(bottom), 233(top), 236-237, 238, 243, 246, 249; T Biegun: 201(bottom);
M Buckner: 234, 242, 251; M Desjardins: 217; M DiGiacomo: 2-3(inset
center), 116(top), 128-129, 130, 133, 140, 142, 143, 144-145, 146-147, 148,
157, 159, 160-161(both), 162(bottom), 180; J Dimaggio/J Kalish: 117, 138-
139, 141(bottom), 174, 176, 184(both), 188; H DiRucco: 240(top), 244;
J Giamundo: 200, 202(bottom), 213, 219, 220(bottom), 228, 250; J Leary:
226, 248(bottom); S Levy: 203; J McIsaac: 229(top), 232, 247, 248(top),
252; D MacMillan: 235(bottom), 239, 245; L Meyer: 222(top), 240(bottom),
241(bottom); H Pichette 209(top); L Portnoy: 131, 178; D Smith 235(top);
Stevens: 230-231; J. Tremmel: 218(top); B Winkler: 205, 211, 218(bottom),
253.

The Bettmann Archive: 2(inset center), 10(top), 19(both), 21(top and
bottom right), 22-23(both), 39(bottom), 51(bottom right), 61, 65, 72-73,
120(top).

Brompton Photo Library: 44, 48(bottom), 101(bottom).

Decathlon Athletic Club: 28(right).

Hockey Hall of Fame, Toronto: 3(inset right), 12(top), 14(both),
15(top and bottom); 16(bottom left), 17(bottom), 18(top right, bottom),
20(top), 20-21, 28(left), 29(both), 30(both), 31(both), 32, 33, 35(both),
36, 37(both), 38(both), 40, 41(both), 45(top left and bottom), 46(both),
47(both), 49(bottom), 50(both), 51(top), 52(both), 53, 54(both),
55(bottom), 56, 57, 59(bottom), 60(both), 62(top), 64, 67(bottom), 69,
70-71, 71(top left), 72(bottom), 73, 74, 75, 77(all three), 78(both), 79,
80(both), 81(both), 84, 85(all three), 86-87(all three), 88, 89, 90(both),
92(top), 93(both), 98, 98(left), 100-101, 102, 104, 106-107(both), 108,
109, 110, 111(both), 112-113, 116(bottom), 118-119, 121(both), 122.

McGill University Archives: 13.

New York Public Library: 10, 11(both).

Public Archives of Canada: 17.

Public Archives of Nova Scotia, Photograph Collection: 12(bottom),
15(center).

Michael Tamborrino: 1, 2-3, 141(top).

TPS/Central Press: 24(top).

TPS/Keystone: 25(top).

United States Hockey Hall of Fame: 18(top left), 68(top).

UPI/Bettmann Newsphotos: 24(center), 26(bottom), 27(top), 34, 39(top),
45(top right), 48(top), 49(top), 51(bottom left), 55(top), 58, 59(top),
62(bottom), 63(all three), 66, 71(right), 76, 92(bottom), 94-95(both),
96(both), 98-99, 100(bottom), 105, 120(bottom).

Acknowledgments
The publisher would like to thank the following people who helped in
the preparation of this book: James Duplacey, Jean Chiaramonte Martin,
Ellen Milionis, Beth Crowell, Design 23, Donna Cornell Muntz, Barbara
Paulding Thrasher, Ralph Dinger, and Mike Tamborrino.

CONTENTS

INTRODUCTION

Back home in New York, they were calling it the 'Blizzard of
'87.' But in Quebec, snowstorms of this magnitude are shrug-
ged off as commonplace. It was through this mere dusting of
the Great White North that my train lurched its way down *La
Belle Province* from Quebec City to Montreal, where I had just
participated in a preparatory meeting for that wonderful two-
game NHL-Soviet series, Rendez-Vous '87. There would be no
air travel that Friday morning and since I was scheduled to be
in Montreal by noon to tape a guest appearance on Dick Irvin's
Hockey Magazine television show, Rail Canada was my only
option.

Wind-driven snow flew by my window, making picturesque
scenes impossible. What better time, I thought, to read that
manuscript my friend Joe Romain had sent me? But as soon as
I began reading, the snow subsided, offering me a view of the
countryside. For a few minutes my attention was divided between manuscript and passing scenery, but before long I was
chewing through the chapters on old-time hockey in the mining towns, the formation of the National Hockey League,
hockey's first golden era, the honor roll of defunct pro franchises, the beginnings of hockey in the United States (a chapter
Joe had asked me to help research) and the NHL in wartime. I
fantasized about the rare, truly memorable photographs that
Romain has since plumbed from the Hockey Hall of Fame
archives to accompany the text. The prospect of this book as an
illustrated chronicle of hockey was exciting.

I peered through the train window and thought of how this
manuscript had propelled me to search for the *real* history of
hockey — I was looking for those legendary young Canadians,
gliding on diamond-hard frozen ponds and streams, bran-
dishing heavily taped sticks with which they would control a
puck with magnetic-like wizardry. How poetic it would be to
witness the duet between printed word and physical specimen.

In New York, there are the dazzling schoolyard basketball
games in which hard concrete replaces hardwood floors,
where to leap for a rebound requires an act of courage. It is the
breeding ground for the pro hoop game. But a pond hockey
game somewhere in Quebec? It sent a shiver down my spine
more chilling than the winter morning.

I recalled the words Andy O'Brien wrote in his masterful
1962 biography of Rocket Richard: 'You'll meet a lot of folks
these days who claim to have spotted stardust on the kid's
shoulders from the first moment he began chasing assorted
morsels of frozen debris on the congealed surface of *Riviere
des Praires* at Montreal's back door.'

Would I spot another Maurice Richard someplace between
Quebec and Montreal? Another Howie Morenz, Jean Beliveau
or Mario Lemieux? Of course it would be just for a mere instant
and I wouldn't really get a good look at him. The tracks would
probably be far from the ice and the moving train, even at its
snow-slow pace, would wipe the scene too quickly from my
vision. But just the very sight, I reasoned, would be enough
for that day. It was not to be. And no wonder. After all, who can
play hockey when a foot and a half of snow lies on the ice?

So enjoy this book, as I did. And keep an eye open for those
kids on the pond. You might see them again in some future
book on the history of hockey.

Stu Hackel
Editor, *Goal* Magazine.

PART I

The Early Years

Who Invented This Game Anyway?

We know who invented the printing press. We know who invented Marxism, basketball, computers and air travel. But do you think we could agree on who invented hockey? A great number of self-appointed Canadian, American and European historians have, with various axes to grind, stated that the game was invented at such and such a time, in such and such a place, and by this or that person. A great deal of this axe-grinding history is what the world of academia refers to, technically, as gobbledygook.

Europeans make reference to various ball-and-stick games played on ice. They show us paintings by artists (as in Pieter Bruegel's *Hunters in the Snow,* for example) from the sixteenth century, in which men on skates and carrying curved sticks chase a ball. Americans make reference to the games played by the Pennsylvania Dutch, while Scots look to the game of hurly as the father of the sport. This game was once banned by the king of Scotland for having caused civil disturbances of considerable consequence. Maritime Canadians point to the British troops who played rough and tumble shinny on Halifax Harbor, while the people of Kingstown, Ontario, make the point that the soldiers in their fair town were much more adept at the game, and can be said to be the true fathers of the sport.

While all this is true, these things have as much to do with ice hockey as Neanderthal hunting has to do with discus throwing. There may be a family resemblance between hockey and whatever happened on Halifax Harbor, frozen Dutch ponds and Scottish head-bashing, but ice hockey, the sport we have come to know and love, came into being in the 1870s, in Montreal, Quebec.

There is a variety of particular versions of this event, but they all share a common element: a folk game was formalized, rules written, standards decided upon and a method of deciding when the game was over was established. This is what we call a sport. Skipping rocks on water is not a sport; the rules are made up to suit the situation. Is the water still or wavy, are the available stones flat or round? This was the way of ice hockey's ancestors. But in Montreal, some standards were met. They are not the same standards we play by today, but they are enough like them

to resemble the game, and records have been kept of when, why, and by whom the standards were changed. This is the mark of a sport, as opposed to a folk game. So most sports historians agree that the birthplace of hockey is Montreal, in the 1870s.

There are at least two versions of this sport's origin that deserve more than passing mention. Most sports historians agree that a Halifax engineer, J G H Creighton, invented the game in 1875, but another, smaller, school of thought gives the nod to another man, who is said to have formalized the game four years later. His name was W F Robertson.

BOTTOM: *A game similar to hockey was played in ancient Greece as seen in this relief.*
BELOW: *Scots participating in the winter sport of 'shinny', their version of hockey.*

RIGHT: *Indians engaged in the sport of lacrosse, which contributed to the development of hockey.*
BELOW RIGHT: *Scottish curling clubs compete in New York.*

ABOVE: *A hockey match takes place at the Victoria Rink in Montreal in 1893.*

BELOW: *JGH Creighton with the 1888 Chebucto team.*

The Creighton Story

JGH Creighton, while attending school in Halifax, Nova Scotia, was a great enthusiast of the games played on the frozen ponds and harbors of Halifax. Soldiers and natives of the community would engage in huge games of hurley, rickey, bandy, shinny, or whatever other name they would give to the ice rumbles which kept them warm and healthy during the long Halifax winters. When Creighton arrived in Montreal in 1872, he missed these raucous exchanges, and proposed to his fellows that they engage in a sort of lacrosse on ice, which proved to be a great failure. A number of attempts were made to concoct a workable game, and they eventually came up with a game which was something like shinny, but was played under modified rugby rules, with one referee and two goal judges. This game was played with such enthusiasm that the nine man teams would play every day of the week at the Victoria skating rink, including those Sundays on which they were able to bribe the caretaker.

The days leading up to 3 March 1875 saw advertisements for a new game, ice hockey, which was to be played at the Victoria rink on that day. One imagines the audience to be comprised of the brothers, friends, wives and sweethearts of the 18 or so gents involved in the game. By this time, a flat, circular piece of wood had replaced the bouncing rubber ball known to former games.

Creighton captained the team chosen from the Montreal football club, while the Victoria skating rink team was headed up by Fred Torrence. The Victoria lineup included the man who is said to have brought ice hockey to Europe: Dr Meagher. The first game scheduled was won by the Montreal team, 2-1, but the second game was cancelled due to a brawl which broke out among the players and the fans, and sent the women spectators rushing, in confusion, from the premises. So this was the birth of ice hockey, and was perhaps the birth of hockey's reputation for being a pretty rough game.

The Robertson Claim

The claim of W F Robertson must be shared with two other men who seem to have had as much to do with the story as Robertson himself. Their names are 'Chick' Murray and 'Dick' Smith. William Galloway, a notable hockey historian from Ottawa, takes great pains to explain that the game played by Creighton and company was little more than recreational figure skating, and has much more to do with shinney than hockey. Bill Fitzel, another notable historian from Kingston, Ontario, believes that the following story bears some semblance to reality, but owes much to 'creative thought expressed years after the fact' by Murray, Smith and Robertson.

After returning from a season in England, Robertson, a student at McGill, met a friend and fellow student, Chick Murray, on Sherbrooke Street on 9 November 1879. Robertson said he had seen some playing in England, and wanted to work up a winter version of it in order to keep the football team fit during the off season. He and Murray devised a set of rules using a rugby football rulebook as a rough guide, and came up with an ice game which used a sort of curved field hockey type of stick, a lacrosse ball with the ends sliced off, and 15-man teams. Dick Smith copied down the rules as dictated by Robertson and Murray, and they had the local Indian tribesman make up the sticks, rented the Crystal skating ring on Dorchester Street and with that, the game of hockey was born.

What is the real story? Who really made up the rules? Did Chick Murray, Robertson and Smith make up their story? All three gave similar accounts to different people at different times. The likelihood that they had a conspiracy of falsehood which lasted 50 or 60 years, well into their old age, is very low indeed. But what of the published and researchable accounts of the 1875 games played by Creighton and company? In order to believe Robertson's claim, we need to discard what cannot be ignored.

The truth probably lies somewhere in between. The historicity of the events would hardly have seemed important to those involved in the events of the day, which leaves us guessing as to the fine details of the development of this fine sport.

The First Games

The McGills playing a hockey match at the Crystal Palace skating rink in Montreal.

Early hockey didn't much resemble the 'shoot and scoot' sort of matches we see on television. For a start there were nine players to a side. Imagine what would happen to a Gretzky where 18 burly brutes charge each other for possession of a converted lacrosse ball bouncing around the uneven and scarred ice surface. During the first few seasons, there were only three teams: the McGills, the Crystals and the Victorias. Everyone was required to remain on-side, no forward passing was allowed, raising the puck was a contraband maneuver and the goalie was required to remain on his feet at all times. A good player meant a good stickhandler.

Before very long, the sides were reduced to seven; the extra man being a rover. This position was pretty much what the name indicates, and the defensive positions were not as we know them. There was a 'point man' who played center ice, and a 'cover point' who played directly behind the point man.

The play during this period was exceedingly rough. Players were equipped with a stick, skates and whatever padding they dared to restrict their movement with. When a skater was checked, it hurt. When a fight broke out, there was no sweater-pulling waltzing, it was a real fight — and as often as not the fans would join right in. If you left the ice, there was no substitution, so no one left the ice without ample cause. And no one was paid for their efforts: with the exception of some under-the-table payola, these men would rough and tumble

for 60 long minutes of bashing and scoring for the love of it.

The new game of ice hockey rapidly caught the imagination of Montreal sports lovers. The matches were well-attended, and every street in town boasted its own hockey team. Montrealers embraced hockey as their own game.

It didn't take long for hockey to spread. To Toronto, Ottawa, Kingston, Quebec City, Renfrew and points both east and west. In 1883 the first known hockey championship tournament took place. The Montreal winter carnival purchased a trophy for 750 dollars (which evidences the committee's devotion to the game) for the 'world championship of ice hockey.' Six teams were entered in the competition. Quebec, Toronto and Ottawa iced teams, as did the original three teams from Montreal: the McGills, the Crystals and the Victorias. The week of 12 February 1883 saw some raw hockey. Thirty games were played, each team playing each other team twice, and the McGills staggered out on top, winning the first ever hockey championship of the world, such as it was.

Sportsmen have always tended to organize themselves in leagues and associations. Hockey is no different. By 1886 hockey clubs from Ontario and Quebec organized the first league: the Canadian Amateur Hockey League. The first 'world champions,' the McGills, were never admitted to this or to any other league. The reason has been lost in the shuffle of antiquity, but this team never competed for the Stanley Cup.

The Early Teams

According to Arthur Farrell, an outstanding player of the time and author of perhaps the oldest book on ice hockey (*Hockey*, published in 1899), the leagues organized and reorganized numerous times during the 1880s and early 1890s. Teams merged, disappeared and reappeared, and players changed allegiances with regularity. A few teams played with some consistency and if only for this reason, are remembered today. Here is a brief look at a few of the teams of the very early days.

The Victorias of Montreal

The Victorias, along with the McGills and the Montreal Football Club, are credited with the invention of the game. These were the teams that honed the rulebook into a workable code of play. They held the championship of the Amateur Hockey Association of Canada from 1884 to 1888, and won the Stanley Cup for four years out of the seven, having successfully defended the Cup five times (twice in 1896). The last winning Victorias team boasts two Hall of Famers: Mike Grant and Graham Drinkwater.

The Montreal Amateur Athletic Association

This may have been the best team of their day. The AAA organized in 1884, and held the Senior Championship Trophy from 1888 to 1894. In 1893, the year Lord Stanley presented the cup, this team, as Senior Champions, became the first recipients of this esteemed prize. In 1896 the Montreal AAA traveled through the northeastern United States, playing the Montreal Shamrocks team in exhibition games. These exhibitions have a lot to do with the spread of the game to the USA.

The Shamrocks

The Shamrocks Hockey Club was not around for very long, but it was good. The Shamrocks took over the Amateur Hockey Association franchise from the Crystals in 1896, and played until 1911, the year they won the Stanley Cup. Three players who are remembered as Hall of Famers are linemates Art Farrell, Fred Scanlan and Harry Trihey (captain).

Victoria Hockey Club of Winnipeg

The Victorias of Winnipeg were organized in 1889, and held the championship of the Manitoba and Northwest Territories

ABOVE: *The Montreal Shamrocks with the Stanley Cup in 1898/99*

LEFT: *The 1893 Montreal Amateur Athletic Association was the first team ever to win a Stanley Cup. They later toured the United States, which helped popularize the game in America.*

RIGHT: *The Victoria Hockey Club of Winnipeg 1894/95 championship team. A great rivalry existed between the Winnipeg Vic's and the Montreal Victorias.*

BELOW RIGHT: *The Wanderers hockey team from Halifax, Nova Scotia, possessed remarkable strength and ability.*
BOTTOM RIGHT: *The 1891/92 Queens College hockey team of Kingston, Ontario, won seven games while losing only one and scored 68 goals while allowing only 13.*

Hockey League until the turn of the century. In 1896 the Winnipeg Vics won the Stanley Cup from their namesakes in Montreal, and lost it again the next season, again to the Montreal Vics. The goaltender for this team, George Merrit, was the first man to wear cricket pads in Stanley Cup play. Donald Bain was one of Canada's finest athletes and one of the great moving influences of this team.

The original challenge took place in Montreal, where confidence in the hometown team was high. The Winnipeggers were on a streak, however, and came up with the big win, 2-0, over the Montreal Victorias. Montreal didn't take very long to respond with a counter challenge. The following season they went to Winnipeg to regain their treasure. This match saw Winnipeggers paying upwards of 12 dollars per seat, and Montrealers huddled in the cold streets as near the telegraph office as their liquor supply would allow. Special arrangements were made to have the 'play by play' of the game telegraphed direct from the arena in Winnipeg. This game was both the highlight of the Winnipeg sporting season, and the disappointment of the decade. For Montrealers things seemed back to normal, and the Montreal Vics would hold the silverware until the Shamrocks took it in 1899.

There were other clubs from those early days whose history has not been forgotten. There was the Toronto Varsity, which became an international force to be reckoned with, the Wanderers of Halifax, an eastern team of remarkable strength and ability, the Quebec Hockey Club, which entered the fray very early on and developed some fine players, and the Queens College hockey team of Kingston, Ontario, whose early games were among the best in the business.

It is not really possible, though try the statisticians and fanatics always will, to compare today's game and players with those of the past, but what we do know is that the game has been one of strength, speed, agility and particular skill from its inception to this day. What made a great player in 1900 is not really what we need on the ice today, though the stamina, determination and ability to work as a team member is certainly common to every stage of the game's development.

The Big Names

Lord Stanley, Baron of Preston

One of the most important figures of the early days of the game was a man who is never known to have donned skates, was not overly fond of cold weather, and who never saw a hockey match until his mid-forties. His name has become, to this day, the most prominent in the sport. The man, of course, is Lord Stanley, Baron of Preston, sixteenth Earl of Derby, Governor General of Canada from 1888 to 1893, and 'father' of the Stanley Cup.

Canada, in 1888, was a dominion, and was under the formal rule of the British monarch. A series of British noblemen filled the role of governor general until 1953, when Vincent Massey, a Canadian, was appointed to the post. Aside from the donation of what has become the oldest trophy competed for by professional athletes in North America, Lord Stanley's governance was not particularly eventful. The following description of Lord Stanley is taken from an Ottawa newspaper.

> Lord Stanley is in the prime of life, medium height, a strong, well-knit frame, a graceful carriage, with something of the look and air of the Prince of Wales when the heir apparent was not quite so stout as he is now. He is fair, with full beard, which is just slightly streaked with grey; has a ruddy complexion, blue eyes, clearly cut features, with aquiline nose. He has a fine, broad forehead, upon which the hair is becoming thin; a genial, winning and frank expression of countenance. His manner is affable; and although his reception, while respectful, was without enthusiasm, he graciously smiled and bowed to those who had gathered to greet him. . . .

LEFT: *Lord Stanley of Preston purchased the Stanley Cup for 50 dollars.*

ABOVE: *The oldest trophy in North America is the Stanley Cup.*

Aside from its being good manners, and good politics, for a governor general to take some interest in the pastimes of his subjects, Stanley had a real liking for the rough and ready game played on the frozen ponds and canals of his new home. In fact his sons (he had eight of them) were said to have been enthusiastic players, and his daughter enjoyed cheering her siblings from the sidelines.

Lord Stanley's parting gesture to the sport was to purchase for 50 dollars, a cup, to be competed for by the best in the country, the winner of the cup being the dominion champions.

J Ambrose O'Brien

John Ambrose O'Brien is one of the great movers and shakers in the history of ice hockey. His personal involvement in the game was relatively short, but his influence is still remembered and revered by historians of the sport.

The son of Michael J O'Brien, a Canadian mining mogul and namesake of the O'Brien Trophy, J Ambrose conducted his sporting affairs with the same shrewdness and sense of purpose he applied to his mining business endeavors, and which made him something of a giant in Canadian business circles.

He was born in the town of Renfrew, Ontario, some 50 miles

from Ottawa. Renfrew may today be no more than a minor whistle stop, but in 1885, Renfrew was a happening place. Along with Cobalt and Hailebury, Renfrew was an important gold, silver, cobalt and nickel mining center. O'Brien played hockey like every other Canadian boy, on the frozen ponds, with the local amateur teams, and unlike every Canadian boy, with the University of Toronto team.

In 1909, when the Renfrew Creamery Kings had become the team to beat in the Ottawa valley district, O'Brien was asked by the team to apply for a franchise in the Eastern Canadian Hockey Association, the premier professional league of the time. O'Brien was refused entry into the league, and, like the entrepreneur he was in his bones, he set about forming his own league; in 1910 the National Hockey Association was born. This league would eventually evolve into the National Hockey League, but in the meantime, O'Brien backed three of the original teams in the league. Along with the Wanderers, who were also refused entry in the ECHA, franchises were granted to Renfrew, Cobalt, Hailebury and Les Canadiens, Jack Laviolette's French Canadian team.

The consternation this new league caused in hockey circles is a subject for another place in this historical sketch, but it should be said that the ECHA was dissolved, the Canadian Hockey Association was formed, and it too was dissolved before that hard winter was through.

O'Brien was serious about his new Renfrew team, the Creamery Kings, and spared no expense to secure some of the finest professional players around. On his roster were at least two Hall of Famers, Lester Patrick and Cyclone Taylor.

The O'Brien interests took the hockey world by storm — they were the force to be reckoned with. This was so much the case that by 1912 the MJ O'Brien Trophy replaced the Stanley Cup as the emblem of championship in the hockey world. But by this time, O'Brien and his interests had cast their eyes elsewhere, and abandoned ice hockey. The Renfrew franchise, which never did win the Cup, became available, along with the Les Canadiens franchise, both of which eventually went to Toronto interests, and merged to become the ancestors of the great Maple Leafs.

John Ambrose O'Brien left a legacy to the hockey world; the National Hockey Association went on to become the National Hockey League, the unrivaled titan of the sport, the O'Brien Trophy has done long and varied service, and the seed which was planted with Jack Laviolette has become the most winning team in professional sport — Les Canadiens du Montreal.

Dr John L (Doc) Gibson

Misunderstandings can cause great potential to go unrealized, but fortunately, some men are able to rise above victimization. Were this not the case, the story of Jack Gibson would be that of a young man barred from playing hockey in the Ontario Hockey Association for accepting money for his achievements on the ice. After a big triumph over the local rival Waterloo team, the Mayor of Berlin, Ontario presented each player with a 10 dollar gold piece to convey his appreciation. The league officials threw the entire team out of the organization for abrogating their amateur status. Along with Jack Gibson, another great was nearly squashed: Arthur Farrell.

ABOVE: *John Ambrose O'Brien started the National Hockey Association which would eventually grow into the National Hockey League.*

LEFT: *The National Hockey Association's MJ O'Brien Trophy which replaced the Stanley Cup for a brief time as the emblem of championship hockey.*

ABOVE LEFT: *Jack 'Doc' Gibson helped bring hockey to the United States by forming the International League.*
ABOVE: *Bruce Stuart played in* *the International League.*
LEFT: *Hugh Lehman, seen here in 1905 as goalie for Vancouver, also played for Doc Gibson.*

Jack Gibson did not like to lose. In 1897, at age 17, Gibson played on a team with two famous Canadian winners, Edward and Joseph Seagram, who made their mark on the world in the distilling business. The team played 15 games, and came up with 14 wins. This was the kind of hockey Gibson liked to play.

Gibson went south to the United States. He studied medicine in Detroit, and in 1901, hung his shingle in the town in Houghton, Michigan. Gibson was not long in establishing his reputation as a big man on the rink. By 1902 Gibson had packed his team with old Canadian teammates, and led his team, the Portage Lakers, through 14 consecutive wins and the championship of the United States.

'Doc,' as he was known, may have maintained his Canadian flavor by bringing in players from his native country, but he soaked up enough of the American entrepreneurial initiative to cast off the charade of amateurism, and was a moving force behind the establishment of the first professional hockey league in the world. The International League was comprised of teams from Portage Lake, Houghton, Calumet, the American and Canadian Soo, and Pittsburgh.

In 1904 Gibson and the Portage Lakers scored 273 goals, while giving up only 48. This season saw the Lakers win 25 of 27 games played, and in exhibition beat the renowned Montreal Wanderers. Unfortunately, Stanley Cup holders would not accept the challenges offered by the International Pro League, so we may never know for certain the real caliber of this northern Michigan powerhouse.

In 1905 Gibson retired from playing hockey but remained active in the league, attracting such players as Joe Hall, Hugh Lehman, George McNamara, Didier Pitre, Babe Siebert and the Stuart brothers, Hod and Bruce.

The specter of professionalism in the sport nearly cost Jack Gibson his future in hockey, but irony being what it is, professionalism has become the mark of greatness in the sport, and it is this that we have come to thank Doc Gibson for.

Early Hockey in Europe

Ball-and-stick games have been popular in Europe for centuries. Those countries which are blessed, or cursed, with winter ice, naturally developed some form of these games for winter entertainment. But ironically, a Canadian (perhaps W F Robertson) is said to have taken from Europe the seed of the game, only to have another Canadian, George Maegher, bring it back in 1894.

The history of the development is rather sketchy but it is clear that the game played in Montreal in the mid to late 1870s had a considerable influence on the progress of European ice hockey history. By 1904 a number of locales in Europe boasted hockey clubs. Included in this group, which played by Canadian ice hockey rules, were Paris, London, Scotland, Switzerland, Belgium and Germany.

The Prince's Club of London, made up mostly of returnees from Canada, was the strongest club during the first decade of the century. During this period, the London club acted as advisors and arbiters of rules and regulations. As more clubs came into being, a need was seen to establish a governing body, with an independent mandate. So in Paris, on 15-16 May 1908, the International Ice Hockey Federation (IIHF) was born. The charter signatories were France, England, Switzerland, Belgium, Germany and Bohemia.

The Europeans were not ready for the new world players. In 1908 the IIHF contemplated a world championship, but backed off the idea for fear that a Canadian team might get itself involved. In fact, in 1910, when the first world championships were held, at Les Avants, Switzerland, the 'Oxford Canadians,' a team comprised of Canadians studying at Oxford University, were allowed to play, but only as exhibitionists — they were not to participate in the competition.

ABOVE: *Students at Oxford University in England enjoy a varsity hockey match in the fog.*
LEFT: *An outdoor ice hockey match played in Stockholm, Sweden. Note the absence of protective equipment, and the rather large goal cage resembling a soccer goal.*

ABOVE: *The Swiss National Team, which is a member of the International Ice Hockey Federation, at the outdoor rink at Davos, Switzerland.*

RIGHT: *In 1920 the Toronto University Varsity Team represented Canada abroad in international competition.*

Teams from Belgium, Switzerland, England and Germany entered the competition, and a sort of round robin was played. The Prince's Club of London won this competition fairly handily, but after the trouncing the Oxford group gave to the other competitors, the first world champions decided not to play them; presumably in order to preserve their reputation as winners.

Most of the northern countries of Europe tended to have hockey teams throughout the early half of the twentieth century, and healthy competition was seen amongst the various amateur teams. Ice hockey was a well-liked sport, but enjoyed nothing like the widespread popularity known in Canada and the United States. As the ranks of Canadians attending European universities increased, many of them played their national sport as members of school clubs. One such team, the Oxford University Club of 1922, saw two rugged skaters who ended up by having a remarkable effect on the future of their homeland: LM (Mike) Pearson became the prime minister, and Rolland Mitchner went on to become the governor general, and a great builder of Canadian sport.

Every year, when half the world was not at war, the IIHF sponsored world championships, and in most years, Canada, followed closely by the United States, won the competitions rather handily. This was fine, if you look from the North

TOP: *The 1937 Swedish team at the world championship ice hockey matches in London, England.*

ABOVE: *The Oxford University hockey team at the Palais de Glace in Paris, France, for a match with the Hockey Club of Paris.*

American perspective, but from the point of view of Europeans, the situation was rather gloomy. It would be difficult to develop a sport at which the Europeans seemed to have little luck.

In 1923 a Swiss medical doctor, Carl Spengler, donated a challenge cup in order to help raise the level of ice hockey play

21

LEFT: *International Ice Hockey Federation matches were often held at the enormous outdoor hockey arena maintained by the Davos Hockey club in Davos, Switzerland.*
ABOVE: *A jubilant Oxford ice hockey team poses for a team photo at the Sportpalost in Berlin, Germany, after defeating the Berlin club 2-1 on 19 December 1931.*

in Europe. The idea seems to have been that more international competition below the level of the European and world championships would be a stimulus to the development of the game. The first competition was held in 1923, and was won by the Oxford University team. In 1928 Clarence Campbell (president of the National Hockey League from 1946 to 1977) played in this competition as a member of the Oxford University Club. The Berlin Hockey Club won this series, defeating the Oxford team and the Davos Hockey Club. The Spengler Cup is still in active service, and holds a rather special place in the world of international competition.

One of the bright lights in European hockey history was John Francis (Bunny) Ahearn, a self-made Irishman from Wexford. Born in 1901, Ahearn was a rather brilliant businessman and diplomat who in 1933 became the secretary of the British Ice Hockey Association. He not only held on to this job for 40 years, but became the vice president of the IIHF in 1955, president in 1957, and remained in one of these two positions until 1975.

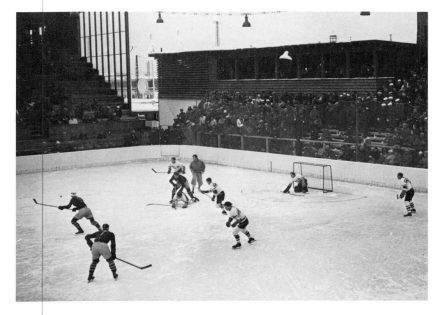

Ahearn founded the semi-professional league in Britain, having organized the Wembley Lions, the Harringay Racers and the Nottingham Panthers. His diplomatic acuity and will to win led him to organize a team of Canadian nationals of British descent for the 1936 Olympics. The team took the gold medal, and caused a bit of bad blood between the Canadian and British ice hockey authorities. In 1977 Bunny Ahearn was recognized by the highest authority known to ice hockey, when he was inducted into the Hockey Hall of Fame.

Throughout the first half of the century, the Canadians and Americans continued to dominate the hockey competitions in which they were involved. It seemed as though nothing would break the spell held by the North Americans. Enter the Soviet team in 1954, when Stockholm, Sweden saw the first top level competition at which the Soviet team was in competition.

The Soviets had been playing a form of 11-man bandy for years, partly because it was fun, but also as a form of winter training for their football team. In 1946 Canadian ice hockey was introduced, and the Soviets lost no time in honing their skills at this game to a very fine edge. By 1954 there were roughly 1400 hockey teams in the country, so clearly there was an interest in this game invented by their northern comrades to the West.

The Soviets, the newcomers to world competition, were the focus of attention, and rewarded the curious by winning game after game, until they met a team which put them to a test, when Sweden tied them at one a piece. During this time Canada had not been sloughing, they had won all their games, and clearly, the world championships were to hang on this one game between the Soviets, the new kids on the block, and the Canadians, regarded as the supreme rulers of the hockey empire. The Soviets swept through the first period with a four-goal advantage (4-0), kept the Canadians guessing through the second (3-1), and by the time the Canadian team began to understand the Soviet play, it was all over (0-1): the final score: Soviets 7, Canada 2.

So much for the Canadian dynasty; Europe had a champion of their own. Sure, other countries had come up with world championship titles before (Germany, USA and Czechoslovakia), but this was different. This team beat Canada decisively at their own game, and left word that they would be a force to be reckoned with. And reckoned with they would be, but not until 1972.

TOP RIGHT: *Great Britain plays Sweden in 1936 at the Olympics in Berlin.*
ABOVE RIGHT: *The US National team defeats Czechoslovakia 2-0 at Garmisch Partenkirchen in the 1936 Olympics.*

RIGHT: *The victorious Canadian team after winning the world title at St Moritz.*
ABOVE FAR RIGHT: *In 1954 the Soviet Union won a gold medal for the first time in Olympic competition at Stockholm, Sweden.*

America

In America, as in most countries of the northern hemisphere, a variety of hockey's forerunners were popular folk games. The Pennsylvania Dutch are known to have played ball-and-stick games on ice from the time of their arrival, and English, Scotch and Northern European immigrants all brought and played their versions of shinney, hurley and related games.

The records of the period shortly following the establishment of ice hockey rules in Montreal are rather scanty, but it is clear that as early as 1885, a game which conforms to the Montreal game was played in Baltimore, Minneapolis and Concord, New Hampshire. Ice polo, a closely associated game, was played earlier than this in New England and in the northern Midwest, and one could safely assume that hockey was played by some border town boys in the years leading up to 1885.

The period between 1875 and 1885 saw a variety of teams hailing from Montreal, Ottawa, Toronto and northeastern Ontario playing exhibitions of the new sport in New York, Boston, northern Michigan and Wisconsin. America watched, liked, and took the sport to heart.

In December of 1894, one of the first indoor ice rinks in North America was established in Baltimore, and what may be the first formalized exhibition of the game played by Amer-

ABOVE: *The Olympic club of San Francisco practicing on a frozen pond in Yosemite National Park in California.*

BELOW: *Columbia University's intercollegiate ice hockey team still plays today in the Metropolitan Hockey League.*

icans was viewed on 26 December of that year. Some American historians believe that this game marks the true birth of the game in the United States.

People of northern countries like ice hockey — Americans, in this respect, are no different from Canadians and Europeans. Once they caught the hockey bug, it became epidemic. The University of Minnesota introduced its first hockey club in 1895, under the tutelage of HA Parkyn, the quarterback of their football team, and yes, a Canuck. This team was quite expert at the game, and on at least one occasion played the Winnipeg Victorias, a cup-winning team (1896).

The following year, 1896, Yale, Cornell, John Hopkins and Maryland all introduced hockey teams, and in the years following Harvard, Brown, Columbia and Dartmouth joined them on the college rinks. By 1899 an intercollegiate league was formed, consisting of Yale, Brown, Harvard, Princeton and Columbia Universities. This was the beginning of what even today is a very healthy hockey league. It would take a good many years (about 80, in fact) before this league would start sending its players, on a regular basis, into the highest ranks of pro hockey, but the record shows a pretty decent level of the sport being played even in the league's infancy.

Meanwhile, in New York City, the Amateur Hockey League (USA) was formed in March of 1896. The games would be played at the old St Nicholas Street Arena, and the four teams, all from New York City, included the St Nicholas Street Hockey Club, which is still in existence some 90 years later.

The first decade of the twentieth century saw hockey explode in the USA. Hockey was organized in Philadelphia, Washington DC, Pittsburgh, St Louis, Minnesota, northern Michigan, New England and North Dakota. And it was during this period that Dr Jack Gibson and his colleagues formed the first ever professional hockey league. At this time in Canada,

ABOVE: *Hink Carson, captain of the Yale University hockey team in 1921.*

BELOW: *The Yale University hockey team at New Haven, Connecticut.*

teams from Duluth (MN), Calumet (MI), Houghton (MI), Sault St Marie (MI), Cleveland (OH), St Paul (MN) and Milwaukee (WI) as charter members. USAHA was affiliated with the Canadian Amateur Hockey Association and the Amateur Athletic Union. This association was plagued with problems, and disbanded after only six seasons of governance, and therefore as there was no governing body, the United States was not represented at the 1928 Olympic hockey tournament. The Amateur Athletic Union of the United States acted as hockey governors from 1930 to 1937, when the Amateur Hockey Association of the United States (AHAUS) was pulled together in New York City by Tommy Lockhart, the first president of America's current amateur hockey governing body.

Hobey Baker

Hobart Amery Hare Baker was one of the finest hockey players ever produced in the United States. He was born in Pennsylvania in 1892, and there learned the skills which would later bring him to prominence in a wide variety of sports. He excelled in golf, swimming, gymnastics and while at Princeton, he made something of a name for himself on the football field.

As a hockey player, Baker was the greatest. It is said that once the puck connected with his stick, it stuck. He played rover, and exemplified the position, sometimes seeming to be in two places at once, one of which was being the delivery end of a goal-scoring drive. He was a very clean player, and has done as much as any player to promote the game in the United States.

Baker went on to be something of a war hero as well, earning a French Croix de Guerre for exceptional valor under fire in 1918. He survived the war, but shortly thereafter died in a plane crash while test piloting a new plane.

His contributions to the game of ice hockey have brought him recognition in both the United States Hockey Hall of Fame, and in the Hockey Hall of Fame in Toronto, where he was one of the first inductees in 1945.

ABOVE: *Hobey Baker was an outstanding player, a war hero and a test pilot.*

RIGHT: *The Hobey Baker Memorial Award, which is presented each year to the outstanding college hockey player.*

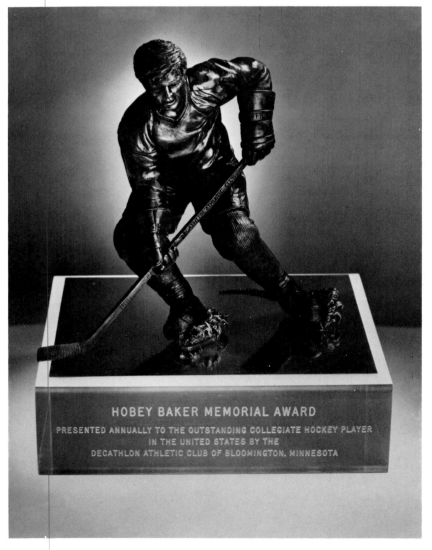

many amateur players were being paid for their services, risking their standing as amateurs, but being well recompensed. The American professional league let the cat out of the bag, and pro hockey began to flourish above the table, so to speak. The league put together very respectable hockey teams. Many say that the Portage Lakers would have taken the Cup, but their frequent challenges went unanswered by the Cup holders in Canada, and it would not be until 1917 that the Seattle Metropolitans would represent the United States as the first team from this country to take the Stanley Cup.

In Philadelphia, on 25 October 1920, the United States Amateur Hockey Association (USAHA) was formed, with

Forwards and Defensemen of the Early Days

Edward (Newsy) Lalonde

The early years of hockey saw many great players. One of the greatest was Newsy Lalonde. Lalonde played center and rover for 20 years for teams which competed for the Stanley Cup. In fact, Lalonde played for teams in no less than nine different leagues, and was often available, at a price, for minor teams which had need of a star player for a decisive game.

He was one of the bad boys of the early days, and had as many fans who loved him as hated him. Whenever he was on the ice, he was the target of any player looking for a scrap. It has been said that Lalonde was disappointed if he finished a game without leaving one of his opponents in need of medical services. But Lalonde was no mere goon. In his 314 career regular season games, he banked some 416 goals, once maintaining a scoring streak for 13 games in 1921, and in 1911, a streak of 11 games. Given these stats, it is surprising that he played on only one Stanley Cup team.

Russell Bowie

Bowie was the centerman of the first decade of the new century. He played his entire career with the Victorias of Montreal, and in his 80 regular season games between 1899 and 1908, scored a remarkable 234 goals, and was the league leader for 5 of his 10 years.

He once scored eight goals against the Shamrocks, in 1907; twice scored seven times; had five six-goal games; 11 five-goal games; and hat trick games were too frequent to bother remembering.

Mike Grant

Credit for the defensive end to end rushes is generally given to Art Ross, but Grant had that move patented very early in his career; Grant's job as a defenceman was to clear the puck from his end; that is, to send the disk toward the rafters, and on to the opposing players' end. Grant got this mixed up, and usually carried the puck clear to the other net. For a defenceman of this era, his 10 goals in 55 games was clearly remarkable.

Sporting a generous moustache through most of his career, he was known as a gentleman on the ice (whatever that might have meant in those bang and clatter games). He played his entire career with the Victorias between 1894 and 1902, and captained his team to four consecutive Stanley Cups. Following his playing career, Grant went on to earn a reputation as a fair and observant referee, and was something of a sight in his stripes and derby hat.

Joseph Hall

Bad Joe Hall was called bad for good reason. He was a dangerous defenceman, and if the stories are true, his rink behavior kept many a forward from challenging him head on. Some of the myths include vicious scraps with Newsy Lalonde, the attack of an official during a Hall-inspired brawl, and conviction in Toronto for his behavior on the rink in that city.

Together with the near giant, Harry Mummery, this defensive duo was known as the 'Bulldogs,' and remains one of the most sobering defensive lines in the history of the game. This

TOP: *Newsy Lalonde with the Montreal Canadiens in 1916 — one of the original bad boys of hockey.*

ABOVE: *Joe Hall in 1917 was a premier defenceman with the Montreal Canadiens.*

pairing of the fearsome Hall with the good-natured Mummery ('Mum') was instrumental in Quebec's two Stanley Cups of the period.

In 1919 in a Cup challenge against Seattle, Joe Hall took ill and died days later of the flu. Due to the influenza epidemic which took Hall's life the series was called off, and that year remains the only one in which the Cup was not awarded.

Duncan (Mickey) MacKay

When Mickey MacKay broke into the PCHA in 1914, his sensational performance at center brought him to the center of western hockey attention: he scored 34 goals in 17 games, and led the league in scoring, a title he would hold twice more during his career.

MacKay was a clean player who avoided infractions, and achieved his fame more through his ability to stickhandle and 'quarterback' than through any antics. He was a great playmaker, and shared the limelight with the remarkable Cyclone Taylor, Frank Boucher and Frank Nighbor. His gentlemanly behavior and team spirit earned him the enviable reputation as one of the good guys of ice hockey.

LEFT: *Joe Malone in 1918 with the Montreal Canadiens.* ABOVE: *Fred 'Cyclone' Taylor seen here in 1915 with Vancouver of the PCHA.*

Joe Malone

Although this look at great players of the period is not intended to be comprehensive, we would be delinquent if mention were not made of Phantom Joe Malone.

Malone was one of the good guys. He played as clean a game as could be expected, and his scoring record has been bested only by Lalonde. He totaled 338 goals in 271 games in the regular season, and 23 in 15 for his years in Stanley Cup playoffs. He captained the Quebec Bulldogs to two cups, and was scoring leader four seasons, including 1918, when Quebec scored in 14 consecutive games with the Canadiens.

Didier Pitre

During the early part of his career, Didier Pitre played defence. He was one of, if not the single fastest skater in this position. In fact, it was Pitre's speed, along with that of his partner, Jack Laviolette, which first inspired the nickname 'the flying Frenchmen' for the Montreal Canadiens.

Pitre played defence for the Canadiens for two years, before manager George Kennedy put Pitre's speed to use on the right wing. His speed, combined with his legendary hard shot, brought him to the fore in the record books. He played on various lines, doing very well, until 1916, when his old defensive linemate and fellow speed demon, Jack Laviolette, was moved to left wing of a forward line with Pitre at right and Newsy Lalonde at center. This remarkable trio led the Canadiens to the first of their many Stanley Cups.

In his 17 seasons, Didier Pitre chocked up 240 goals in 282 regular season games, and earned himself a berth in the Hockey Hall of Fame.

Arthur Ross

Art Ross was a defensive player, and as his career shows, he was as tough to deal with off the ice as on it. His playing career spans the years 1905 to 1918, and more particularly, spans that period of organization when leagues and teams came and went with some regularity. Part of this may well have been due to Ross' unbending dedication to the rights of ice hockey players. When the club owners banded together to limit the salaries of players, and hence keep the lion's share of gate receipts to themselves, Ross protested first privately, and when that did not work, went to the press with his side of the story. He threatened to organize a new league, and the owners relented somewhat, but were not prepared to share the riches with those who earned them. Ross became something of an Allan Eagleson, and negotiated on behalf of his fellow puck shooters. In 1915, when the Wanderers' management limited players' salaries to 600 dollars, Ross began signing players to options in a new league. Ross was banned from organized hockey for being the vanguard of the rising proletariat of hockey players, but as the players with which he had tampered were also guilty of tampering, and made up a large portion of the league, Ross had to be reinstated.

Ross was a big man on the ice as well. He played a clean, but tough, game and is remembered for his end to end rushes as early as 1907, when playing with Si Griffis on the Kenora Thistles. With Kenora, he won the Stanley Cup in 1907, and the following year he played with the Montreal Wanderers. For a defenceman, he did pretty well in the record book: 85 goals in 167 regular season games, and 6 in 16 in playoff encounters. For reasons unknown to us, a trophy for the most goals scored in a season was given his name, and is still a hotly contested piece of silverware in the National Hockey League.

LEFT: *Art Ross during his playing career around 1905.*

BELOW: *The 1906/07 Stanley Cup champion Kenora Thistles.*

Early Goaltending

Perhaps the single most important man on the ice is the goaltender. He is not given the limelight in the way that a pitcher in baseball is, but in many ways, the two serve similar roles. When the pitcher makes a mistake, the result is often pivotal. When the goaltender makes a mistake, the outcome is almost always decisive.

Early goaltenders had this same mixed blessing, but they did not have the equipment or maneuverability of the present-day cageminders. For one thing, they had no equipment which distinguished them from the other players. They may have rolled newspapers or magazines to protect their more vulnerable body parts, but sticks, gloves and skates were the same as those of their fellows.

At first glance, this may seem suicidal, but it must be remembered that the slapshot, backhand shot, and 'raised shot' were not legal maneuvers. The job of the goalie was to stay between the goal markers and check incoming forwards. He was not to kneel, lay on the ice, or catch the puck with his hands. One wonders how, given this scenario, goaltenders lived through a game, let alone made many saves. But good goaltenders there were, and they were recognized as special from early on.

BELOW: *Clint Benedict seen here wearing a leather mask to protect his broken nose.*

RIGHT: *Georges Vezina played goal for Montreal for 15 years, until his death.*

Georges Vezina

Perhaps the most revered goalie from the early days was a man called the Chicoutimi Cucumber. Georges Vezina, namesake of the Vezina Trophy, played the great standup game. Never known to take a dive, or do anything particularly showy, he played 15 years of pro hockey between the years 1911 and 1926, all of his career with the Montreal Canadiens. He played on five championship teams, and took the Stanley Cup on two occasions.

Clint Benedict

One of the great reformers of the goalies' role was Clint Benedict. Benedict squirmed and rolled about the ice, putting on a great show, but in the process, broke the standing rule so often that the rule was changed in 1917 to accommodate his antics (in fact, this rule was in place in the Pacific Coast Hockey Association since 1912). When Howie Morenz's powerful shot broke Benedict's nose, another modification was made to the goaltender's appearance: he appeared in the following game sporting the leather mask for which he is now famous. Benedict wore the mask until his nose was healed, and goalie masks did not make their reappearance until Jacques Plante began his mask development in the late 1950s.

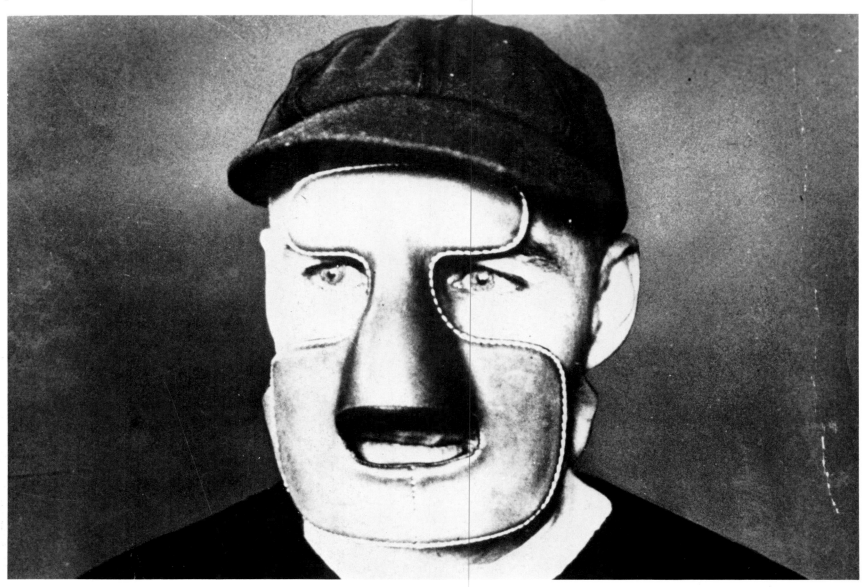

John Ross Roach

Although never inducted into the Hockey Hall of Fame, John Ross Roach was one of the bright stars of his era. He played for 14 years, posting 56 shutouts, and a lifetime average of 2.54 goals against. In 1932 Roach was sold to the Detroit franchise for 11,000 dollars, and was in that year the first Detroit player to be selected for the all-star team.

'Happy' Harry Holmes

'Happy' Harry Holmes was a much respected goaltender whose goals-against record was second only to Clint Benedict's. He played on seven championship teams, and served on four Cup winners, including America's first recipients, the Seattle Metropolitans, in 1917.

Fred Brophy

One great goalie we should not ever forget is Fred Brophy. He may not have been the greatest goalie of all time, but he will be remembered as the only goalie to score two goals while playing the position. On 18 February 1905, while playing with Montreal in a game against (who else?) Quebec, Brophy took possession of the disk, cruised the length of the ice and incredibly racked one in against his opposing goalie, Paddy Moran. Then, as if to prove it was not a fluke, in March of the following year, Brophy once again blocked a shot, left his crease, eluded Russell Bowie, Joe Eveleigh and the rest of the Victoria team (no easy feat even for a forward) and slipped one by the much dismayed goalkeeper Nathan Frye, to the delight of the roaring crowd. So who says Bobby Orr is the father of the rushing defenceman?

These are some of the great men of the web from the early days of the game. The art of the goaltender has developed substantially since these men guarded the nets (today, some goalies talk to the posts, *that's* progress), but it still requires courage, stamina, incredible reflexes and a casual disposition towards one's life and limb.

ABOVE: *Paddy Moran was the unlucky goalie for Quebec who Fred Brophy, the opposing goalie, scored upon in 1905.* RIGHT: *Harold 'Hap' Holmes registered 11 shutouts in 1927/28 with the Detroit Cougars and was in goal for the Seattle Metropolitans in 1917 when they became the first US team to win the Stanley Cup.*

LEFT: *John Ross Roach, seen here with the Toronto St Pats in 1926, posted 56 shutouts in his career.*

The Pacific Coast Hockey Association

BY RON BOILEAU

When one looks at the development of the game of ice hockey, one has to devote considerable space to Frank and Lester Patrick and their PCHA. While in their mid-twenties, the Patricks had been stars in the Canadian Amateur Hockey League, the Eastern Canadian Amateur Hockey Association, and in the only existing pro hockey circuit, the National Hockey Association. Being pretty bright boys, they saw that the real money was to be made on the management side of the rink, and so with the money from the sale of their father's lumber mill in the Nelson, British Columbia area, they set out to gamble their fortune on the establishment of a western hockey league. Now, this was no small gamble: most people in the West had never even seen hockey, so there was no 'market study' for the project. The climate in the populated areas of British Columbia was wonderfully suited to human habitation, which was fine, but it was for the same reasons not suited to the primary ingredient of ice hockey: ice. This meant that artificial ice surfaces would be the first bridge they would have to cross. The only existing artificial ice surface in North America was in the St Nicholas Arena in New York City, so the experts were brought west, and two arenas were built. The Willows Arena in Victoria held 2500 spectators and cost 110,000 dollars to build, and the Denman Street Arena in Vancouver cost 275,000 and would seat 10,500 fans. For 1911, this was big

business and by today's conservative standards, was a gamble of outlandish proportions. How would they get the uninitiated masses into the 13,000 seats the Patricks paid so dearly for?

How? They raided the National Hockey Association, that's how. They had played in the East, and had a pretty good idea of who was who in the league, and who might be bought. Many of the players they gleaned were former teammates, opponents and upstarts. These bright stars would fill the seats with westerners who had heard of, but never seen, these legends of the ice from back East.

On 2 January 1912, the first professional ice hockey game on artificial ice was played in Victoria, between the New Westminster Royals and the Victoria Senators. Artificial ice was not the only first this league brought to the sport; the players appeared on the ice wearing large numbers on their backs, the first time this had been done in any sport. Innovation is the primary reason for the importance of this league, as the Patricks had a knack for bringing ideas to fruition.

The 1912/13 Vancouver Millionaires hockey team of the PCHA played in arenas built by the Patrick brothers, who started the league. Their gamble paid off in 1915 when they won the Stanley Cup from the Ottawa Senators of the NHA.

This first season of hockey's premier in the West saw three teams compete: the Victoria Aristocrats, the New Westminster Royals and the Vancouver Millionaires. New Westminster would play on Vancouver ice until their own arena was built two years hence. The PCHA was off to a grand start, and the Patricks' gamble had paid off. People flocked to see the games both in Vancouver and in Victoria, and the chimes of the ticket sellers' registers proved that hockey had arrived in the West.

The 1914/15 season saw the league expand into the United States, with a team from Portland taking the place of New Westminster. In 1915/16, a team from Seattle entered the league, and was joined the following year by a team from Spokane, Washington.

In 1914 the Stanley Cup trustees were finally convinced to introduce a competition between the PCHA and the NHA champions for the Cup. This was in the best interest of the game, and the competition between the leagues, East and West, was fierce. By 1915 the upstart hockey league had shown its mustard, and took the NHA championship Ottawa Senators three games to none in Stanley Cup competition. All three games were played in Vancouver, and all hell broke loose in the West. Not only did the westerners take the Cup, but they did so with such outstanding scores (2-6, 3-8, 3-12) that every westerner worthy of the name became a hockey fanatic.

In 1917 the trail of the Stanley Cup would take a dramatic turn to the South: an American team went home with the prize. Four games were played in late March of the year, between the Montreal Canadiens and the Seattle Metropolitans. The Canadiens blasted into town with an 8-4 victory over

BELOW: *The 1912/13 Victoria Senators played the first professional game on artificial ice. Lester Patrick is second from the right.*

RIGHT: *Frank Foyston of the 1917 Seattle Metropolitans.*

WESTERN CHAMPIONS
1924-25

WORLD CHAMPIONS
1924-25

HARRY MEEKING

HAROLD HART

"HAPPY" HOLMES

CLEM LOUGHLIN
CAPT.

FRANK FREDRICKSON

"SLIM" HALDERSON

"JOCKO" ANDERSON

GORDON FRASER

FRANK FOYSTON

MANAGER
LESTER PATRICK

JACK WALKER

WALLY ELMER

VICTORIA COUGARS

W.C.H.L. CUP

STANLEY CUP

the Mets. The hometown fans' support for their boys never faltered, as they had seen Frank Foyston, Cully Wilson and Bernie Morris work before. The Mets replied with three decisive victories (6-1, 4-1, 9-1), and kept Montreal's beloved cup stateside. These teams would face each other in 1919, when the great influenza epidemic cut short the series, and no Stanley Cup was awarded in that fateful year.

The PCHA would hold the cup on one more occasion. In 1925 the Montreal Canadiens would travel west again to face the Victoria Cougars in a four-game series. Victoria would hold the Habs to one victory, and would take the remaining three games, and the Stanley Cup, for their own.

Three Stanley Cup wins, however triumphant this may appear, is not really the measure of the value of the PCHA in the development of the game. In the 15-year history of the league, it fostered a great number of innovations to the rules of play, the statistical record keeping, and the awarding of franchises. Some of the more important changes brought about by the Patricks have included the drawing of blue lines and allowance of forward passing in the center zone, allowing the players to kick the puck (though not into the net), allowing the goaltender to leave his feet, the awarding and recording of assists, the delayed penalty, the playoff system, the farm system of player and team development, penalty shots, the tactic of changing forward lines on the fly, counted shots on goal, and the awarding of a franchise outside of Canada.

In 1922 the PCHA began to play an interlocking schedule with the Western Canada Hockey League, who had teams in Edmonton, Regina, Calgary and Saskatoon. This league had existed in various forms for a few years, but in the 1921/22 season they joined the pro ranks, and shortly thereafter

LEFT: *The Stanley Cup champion Victoria Cougars of 1924/25 would move to Detroit and eventually become the Redwings.*

BOTTOM LEFT: *Frank Patrick seen in 1912 with the Vancouver Millionaires of the PCHA.*
BELOW: *Lester Patrick would go on to manage and coach the New York Rangers to three Stanley Cup victories.*
RIGHT: *Dick Irvin captained the 1926 Portland Rosebuds.*

shared a schedule with the Pacific Coast boys. In the final two season of the PCHA existence, the two leagues merged to form one six-team league.

After the 1925/26 season, the Patricks folded the league and sold the players to the National Hockey League for the whopping sum of 300,000 dollars. This was quite a price, but the PCHA had seen some great players. Of the 170 men who laced their skates for the Patricks, 35 went into the Hockey Hall of Fame. Cyclone Taylor, Mickey MacKay, Si Griffis, Jack Adams, Frank Nighbor, Didier Pitre, Bullet Joe Simpson, Red Dutton, Dick Irvin and Mickey Ion are among the men who made their names with this innovative and exciting league. Frank Patrick went into the gold mining business and lost most of what he made in the great game, and Lester went on to become a force with the National Hockey League, as a player, coach, manager and league official. When one considers the bold new changes the Patricks made to the game, it is fitting that the current National Hockey League has both a division and a trophy to mark the trail blazed by these remarkable men.

Boom Town Hockey

BY JOHN SABLJIC

The modern hockey fan, accustomed to big city teams like the New York Rangers and Montreal Canadiens, might find it difficult to believe that the all-time list of Stanley Cup challengers includes teams from Kenora, Haileybury, Cobalt and Dawson City. With a combined population of 17,198, they would be 302 bodies short of filling Madison Square Garden!

During the first 15 years of the century, these places were boom towns, made rich by gold and silver mining. They popped up in the Canadian wilderness, attracting tough, hard-working young men with promises of good wages and a rough and tumble life style. Finding themselves in the middle of nowhere, they improvised their off-hours entertainment as best they could. Along with drinking, gambling and fighting, hockey filled the need for exciting entertainment. Wealthy mine owners could gain popularity and fame by providing their town with a winning team. Because most of the top players of the day signed short-term contracts, there was always plenty of talent available to those willing to pay for it, and great teams could be built overnight and dismantled just as quickly. The miners soon developed fanatical loyalties toward their local teams, betting thousands on the outcome of a single game.

The first pro circuit, the International Pro Hockey League, was born in the mining region of northern Michigan. Most Canadian mining communities, from Trail, British Columbia to the coal mines of Nova Scotia, also became hotbeds of hockey, but it was in the small copper-mining town of Houghton, Michigan, that the professional game was born. It was there, in 1904, that Dr JL Gibson, a dentist and former Canadian hockey player, assembled a group of paid imports to play exhibition games against the neighboring towns. The Portage Lakers, as his team was known, dominated the local talent so

completely that the other towns signed their own stars. Thus in 1904/05, the first pro season was underway. The first Canadian city to boast a professional team was Sault Ste Marie, Ontario which was an original member of the International Pro Hockey League. The other league members included Pittsburgh, Sault Ste Marie, Michigan and Calumet, Michigan.

The league folded in 1907, mainly because the small arenas couldn't generate enough money to offset the payroll and traveling expenses. While it lasted, it entertained the miners with a fast and violent brand of hockey and provided employment for some of the biggest stars of the day. Cyclone Taylor, Newsy Lalonde and Hod Stuart, Hall of Famers all, started their illustrious professional careers there. With the league's demise, these and many other excellent players became available, hastening the professionalization of the major Canadian leagues.

Like hired gunslingers in the Old West, top players would sell their services to the highest bidder, become instant local heroes and then slip away to another town to start the process all over. Art Ross was given 1000 dollars per game by Haileybury during the 1908 Upper Ottawa Valley League Championship. Renfrew paid Fred 'Cyclone' Taylor over 5500 dollars for a 12-game season, making him the most highly paid professional athlete of his time on a per-month basis.

The owner of the Renfrew Creamery Kings was John Ambrose O'Brien, a local silver tycoon. In his determination to win the Stanley Cup, he squandered a fortune to sign superstars like Taylor, Les Patrick, Newsy Lalonde and Sprague Cleghorn. When his bid for a franchise in the prestigious ECHA was turned down, he almost single-handedly formed the National Hockey Association. During the league's first year of operation, O'Brien financed three of the league's original five teams. So successful was the NHA that the old circuit quickly folded, forcing its team owners to apply to the same man they had so recently rejected.

The Kenora Thistles also entertained Stanley Cup ambitions, but they were less willing to go broke in the trying. Their solution was to 'rent' stars when they needed them. In January of 1907, with Art Ross on loan from Brandon, they beat the Montreal Wanderers for the Cup. Despite attempts by the Wanderers to block any further roster stacking, the Thistles had acquired two more 'rent-a-stars' by the time the two teams met again in March. They were Alf Smith and Harry Westwick from the Ottawa Senators. But the ringers weren't enough to beat the Wanderers. The Cup returned with them to Montreal and Kenora sank back into hockey obscurity.

Of all the early mining teams, the most exotic and spectacularly unsuccessful was Dawson City. Their moment in the spotlight came in January of 1905 when they challenged the mighty Ottawa Silver Seven for the Cup. Ottawa was considered the strongest team of the era while the Klondikers were a collection of nonentities, has-beens and rank amateurs. But Dawson had won the Yukon championship, a feat which apparently convinced them that they had the makings of greatness. After a 24-day, 4000-mile journey costing 6000 dollars, they arrived in Ottawa. The following day, they played their first game against the Stanley Cup champs. The result, a 9-2 loss at the hands of the Silver Seven, did nothing to dampen the optimism of Klondike Joe Boyle, the Dawson manager. 'We've got the team and will show Ottawans the real thing tonight. . . . We have a good chance to win the Cup,' he said, the morning before the second game. Even after the 23-2 annihilation they suffered that Monday afternoon, he was able to say, 'nevertheless, it was a good game. . . .'

LEFT: *As boom towns sprang up across Canada in the 1880s, hockey became a popular way for many to entertain themselves. Eventually mining companies developed pro teams as a way of gaining popularity and fame.*

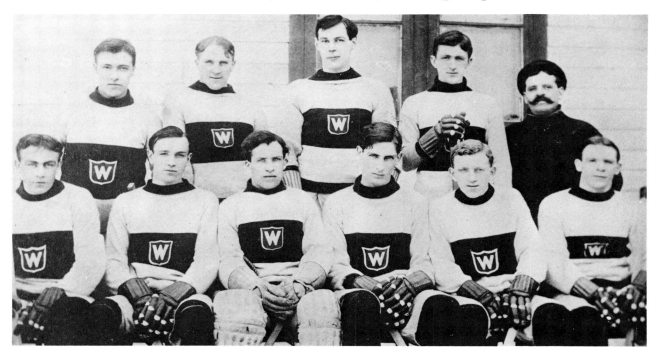

RIGHT: *The 1907 Stanley Cup champion Montreal Wanderers beat the Kenora Thistles.*
BELOW: *Hockey being played in the mining town of Dawson City in the Yukon in 1900. Dawson City would play for the Cup only once in 1905 and lose to the Ottawa Senators.*

PART II

The Early Pro Years

1920-1945

Defunct Teams of the Period

Most hockey fans refer to something called 'The Original Six,' by which they mean the six teams that played during the golden era of the current fans' short memory. There never was an 'Original Six.' There were four teams in the original NHL, and although the league is a fairly stable organization today, there has been a considerable amount of coming and going among franchises throughout the history of the league.

One of the most volatile times in the league's history, aside from the World Hockey Association wars, was that period between the mid-1920s and the late 1930s.

The Ottawa Senators, 1884 to 1934

The Ottawa Senators is probably the oldest hockey club in English Canada. We are certain that they are one of the oldest, as they played in the 1884 Montreal Winter Carnival Series. The Hockey Hall of Fame and Museum in Toronto holds some beautiful photographs of this team, dating as early as 1896, when Harry Westwick, Harvey Pulford and Alf Smith were in the lineup, and Arthur Farrell makes reference to them in his book *Hockey,* published in 1899.

Ottawa, as the national capital, had served as an ambassador of Canada's national sport since the earliest days of the game. The sons of Lord Stanley are known to have learned the game in Canada, and taken it to the royal ice rinks of the British aristocracy. The heyday of the Ottawa Senators must surely have made a great impression on the foreign guests and dignitaries who were introduced to ice hockey at Ottawa's Dey's Rink.

The Silver Seven, as they came to be known, were no fly-by-night operation in the National Hockey League. They entered the league in 1917 directly through its predecessor, the National Hockey Association, and took nine Cups before sending the franchise stateside, to St Louis in 1933, when the reality of the Great Depression left its imprint on the hockey world.

BELOW: *The 1893 Ottawa Senators, also known as the Silver Seven.*
RIGHT: *Bill Beveridge in goal for the Ottawa Senators in 1933.*

FAR RIGHT: *Frank Clancy would help the Senators win the Stanley Cup, the O'Brien Trophy and the Prince of Wales Trophy in 1927.*
BELOW RIGHT: *The 1927 Ottawa Senators.*

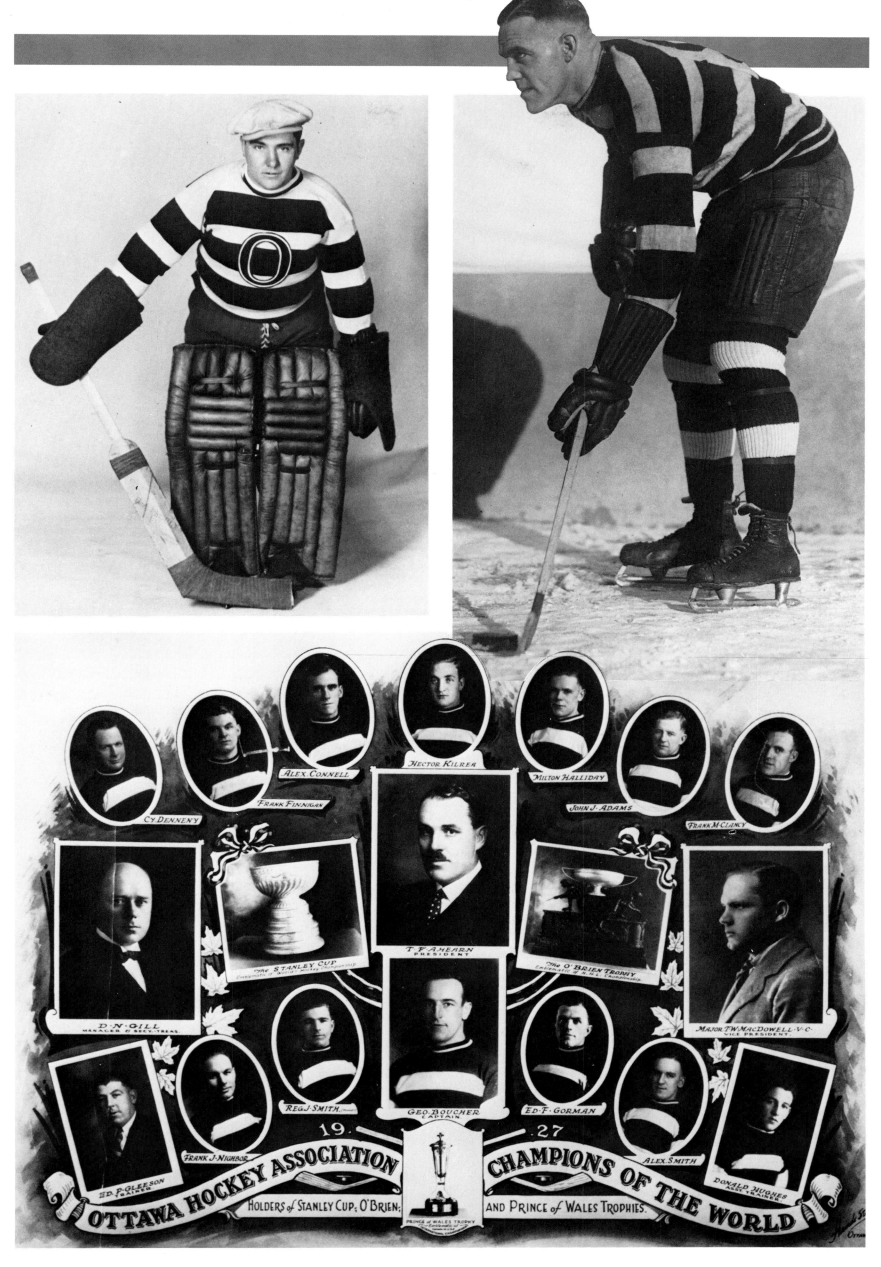

Cy Denneny
Frank Finnigan
Alex Connell
Hector Kilrea
Milton Halliday
John J. Adams
Frank M. Clancy

D. N. Gill
MANAGER & SECY-TREAS.

The Stanley Cup
Emblematic of World's Hockey Championship

T. F. Ahearn
PRESIDENT

The O'Brien Trophy
Emblematic of N.H.L. Championship

Major T. W. MacDowell V.C.
VICE PRESIDENT

Ed. P. Gleeson
TRAINER

Frank J. Nighbor

Reg J. Smith

Geo. Boucher
CAPTAIN

Ed. F. Gorman

Alex Smith

Donald Hughes
ASST TRAINER

19 27
OTTAWA HOCKEY ASSOCIATION CHAMPIONS OF THE WORLD
HOLDERS of STANLEY CUP; O'BRIEN; AND PRINCE of WALES TROPHIES.

PRINCE of WALES TROPHY

The Montreal Wanderers

The Montreal Wanderers were one of the original teams who threw in their lot with the NHL in 1917. They had been around as an organization since 1903, when they played in the Federal Amateur Hockey League. In the first season of operation, the Wanderers' arena burned to the ground, leaving the Wanderers truly wandering, and they had to drop out of play after only six games (four were played, two were defaults). The first year of NHL play was conducted between three teams: the Canadiens, Toronto and the Ottawa Senators.

The Pittsburgh Pirates

This team began their history as the Yellow Jackets, a team of Canadian and American amateurs who were pulled together by Lionel Conacher when he went to Pittsburgh to play football and study at Dusquane University. When the league granted the franchise, the Yellow Jackets, as the premier team of the area, were offered the chance to go pro.

The Pirates entered the league in 1925, operating out of the Dusquane Gardens in Pittsburgh, Pennsylvania, on what is now the campus of Dusquane University. The team was coached by Odie Cleghorn, who instituted the three line system. This advance over the traditional approach of icing the top five skaters for the bulk of the match led to a faster game, and brought the Pirates into Stanley Cup play twice in their five-year history. The Pittsburgh team was not one of the star-studded teams of the era, although they did employ Lionel Conacher, Canadian athlete of the half century, Mickey MacKay of Pacific Coast Hockey League fame, and such minor stars as Hib Milks, Tex White and Toots Holloway.

The Philadelphia Quakers

In 1930 Pittsburgh could not support their franchise due mainly to the Great Depression. The franchise was relocated in Philadelphia, and given the name 'Quakers' after the religious

LEFT: *The 1925/26 Pittsburgh Pirates instituted the three-line system, creating a faster game.*
BELOW LEFT: *Herb Drury in 1931 with the Philadelphia Quakers, formerly the Pittsburgh Pirates.*

BELOW: *Nels Stewart of the Montreal Maroons held the all-time scoring record until Maurice Richard surpassed it.*
RIGHT: *The 1936/37 Montreal Maroons, who were coached by Tommy Gorman and Frank 'King' Clancy.*

community of the Pennsylvania countryside.

This one-year blip on the screen of NHL history nearly set a record for futility. They won four of their 44 game schedule, tied four, and lost 36 big games. Cooper Smeaton, the Hall of Fame referee, was behind the bench, but was unable to make a silk purse of a sow's ear. He was not to have a second chance in the city of brotherly love, and the team folded after this one disastrous year. Philadelphia would not see National League caliber hockey for another 37 years, when the Flyers brought an explosion of talent to this great hockey town.

Montreal Maroons

The Maroons entered the league in 1924 and iced respectable teams for some 13 years. They always had a reputation for being a tough checking team, and not afraid of the penalty box. The 'S' line of the early thirties, comprised of Babe Siebert, Hooley Smith and Nels Stewart, averaged 200 penalty minutes in their first three seasons of play. The club took two Stanley Cups during their tenure with the league, and participated in Cup play in all but three of their years.

The Maroons were coached by some big hockey names such as ex-Ottawa newspaper man Tommy Gorman (and who knows hockey better than ex-newspaper men?), gritty National Leaguer Eddie Gerard, and in 1938, were kept in line by Frank 'King' Clancy. Nels Stewart, one of the stars of the Maroons' early years, finished his career with the all-time record for goal scoring, only to be eclipsed by Maurice 'The Rocket' Richard some ten years later. Other stars who graced the lineup of Maroons' history include George Boucher, Alex Connell, Dave Trottier, Reg Noble, Clint Benedict and Carl Voss.

Montreal was and is a great hockey town. The rivalries between the Canadiens and the Maroons were intense. Though the English-French divisions, apparent in much French Canadian culture, were not at the heart of the rivalry, the Maroons tended to be supported by English, while 'Les Habitants' were the favorite of the Quebecois. As they shared the Montreal forum, the team support was bound to get hot from time to time.

Rather fittingly, the last home game the Maroons played was against their great rivals, the Montreal Canadiens. The team was depleted by the retirement of many of its big stars, and rumblings of war in Europe caused financial backers to balk. The team did not transfer the franchise, but let it die a respectable death at the close of the 1938 season.

The Quebec Bulldogs

The Quebec Bulldogs came into existence before the turn of the century, probably in 1893, and held fort in Quebec City until 1920, when the franchise was moved to Hamilton, Ontario, where they became another sort of animal, the Tigers. During their reign, they took two Stanley Cups in 1912 and 1913, and although they were involved in the National Hockey League from the start, they played only during the 1920 season.

The biggest skating star to play with the Bulldogs was Phantom Joe Malone. Malone was a great goal scorer. In 16 pro seasons, he scored 338 goals, and in one season, while with the Canadiens, he potted 44 goals in 22 games for a 2.2 average, a record still unbroken even by the great Gretzky. Other great men to don the crest were Bert Lindsay, father of 'Terrible Ted,' the infamous Bad Joe Hall, Russell Crawford, Jack Marks and Eddie Oatman.

The Hamilton Tigers

The great year of the Tigers was 1925, when they finished first in the National Hockey League. A close race with the Toronto St Pats left Hamilton with 39 points to Toronto's 38. The team was led by Billy Burch at center, with Roy and Wilfred Green on the wings and Jumpin' Jake Forbes tending the net. The players had signed two-year contracts the previous year, for 24 games per season. When the schedule was increased by six games, the owners of the club would not give the players compensation for the six extra games, and the players threatened to strike the Stanley Cup series. They asked for 200 dollars per man, and were refused. When it became apparent that the players were firm in their strike, president Frank

Calder declared that the second and third place Toronto and Montreal teams would playoff for the league championship, and the Hamilton franchise would be passed over. Where is Alan Eagleson when you need him?

LEFT: *The 1912/13 Stanley Cup champion Quebec Bulldogs.*
ABOVE LEFT: *Red Dutton played wing for the New York Americans in 1933.*
ABOVE: *The 1933 New York Americans became the* Brooklyn Americans in 1941/ 42, and folded after the 1942 season.
RIGHT: *Roy Worters played goal for the New York Americans, and recorded 13 shutouts in 1928/29.*

The New York Americans

When the Hamilton team was left out of the final series in 1925, it became clear that the franchise was unsupportable in that city, and it was sold to American interests in New York. In 1925/26, the Hamilton team became the New York Americans. Sporting the most colorful uniforms the game had yet known, they took to the Madison Square Garden ice with a lineup which included Billy Burch, Wilf and Red Green, and Jake Forbes in net. That first year they won 12 of 36 games, finishing fifth of seven NHL teams. Not too impressive for a team that finished first in the previous season.

Over the course of the next 15 seasons, the Amerks entered playoff competition five times, but never came up with the ultimate hockey triumph. Over the course of their 16-year history, this notable team, headed up by the great Tommy Gorman, paid the salary of some remarkable men. Among them were Red Dutton, Roy Worters, Leo Reise, Bullet Joe Simpson, Laton (Hap) Emms and Lionel Conacher. Old-timers remember this team for the astounding 1938 quarterfinals fought against the Amerks' mortal rivals, the New York Rangers. In the best of three series the Americans came out on top after three overtime periods in the decisive third and final game.

The Brooklyn Americans

In the 1941-42 season, in order to develop a local following, the New York Americans team changed its name to the Brooklyn Americans. The name change did nothing to improve the fortune of this colorful, but financially troubled, franchise. After only one year of play as Brooklyn, it was agreed that the team would suspend operations for the duration of the world war, at which time Red Dutton was to rekindle the Amerks' existence.

At the conclusion of the war, the league decided that one New York franchise would suffice, and the grand tradition that began in Quebec in the very early days of the game, came to an end. Following this period in the development of the league, a new era of stable franchises set the tone for the emergence of individuals who would go on to excel, and open a new chapter in the annals of the game.

BELOW: *Red Dutton as manager of the Brooklyn Americans in 1942, their last year in existence.*

RIGHT: *Fred Thurier played for the Brooklyn Americans in 1942.*

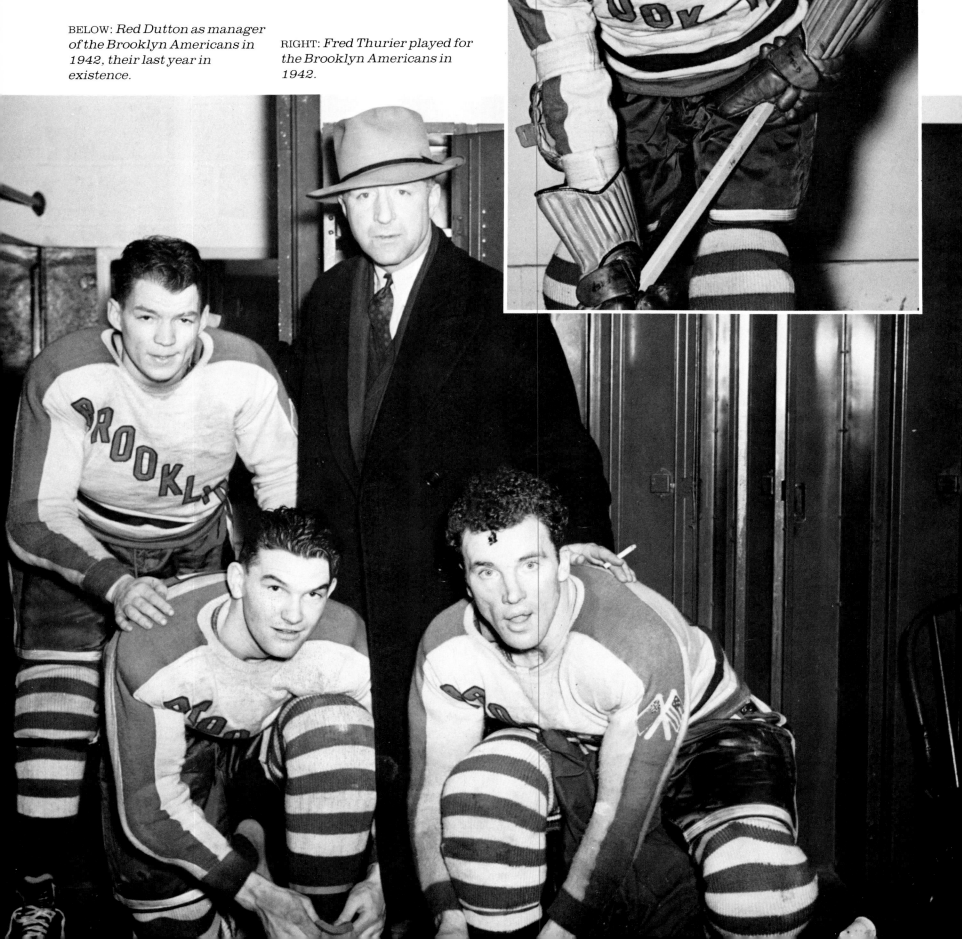

Bailey, Shore and the All-Star Games

The history of all-star competition in ice hockey is pretty sentimental. Hockey players are a rough and tumble group of individuals, but they have tended to be a loyal bunch both on and off the ice. As the case of the Bailey-Shore incident indicates, they might be chopping each other to bits with lethal sticks one night, and putting their all into a benefit for one of their own the next.

Reports of the game played at Boston Garden on the night of 12 December 1933 relate a tale of perhaps the worst hockey spectacle ever recorded. The game was not ice hockey, but something more akin to a barroom brawl. The Boston Globe reported that the officials were clearly inefficient, and the play was the most hatchet-type game ever to be played in Boston.

The two men behind the benches were Art Ross and Conn Smythe. To understate the case, they hated each other with a passion that has become legend in the annals of hockey. In the days of such managers, a rival between the front offices meant feisty matches on the ice. This night has been attributed to the feud between these two colorful gents on more than one occasion.

The Globe reports that the officials let the game get way out of hand almost from the first. A series of jangles between King Clancy, Dit Clapper, Baldy Cotton, Joe Lamb, Red Horner, Bob Gracie and Ace Bailey broke out almost from the start, and the game went downhill from there. Clancy checked Eddie Shore at the Bruins' blue line, spinning Shore over his knee and leaving him dazed on the glass. Clancy then headed for the Bruins' end, carrying the puck. Bailey was skating backwards toward his blue line, in anticipation of the shifting play,

BELOW LEFT: *Frank 'King' Clancy instigated the Ace Bailey – Eddie Shore incident by checking Eddie Shore.* ABOVE: *Conn Smythe, owner and manager of the Toronto* Maple Leafs, served as a major during the second world war. BELOW: *Eddie Shore played 13 seasons for Boston and was elected to the Hall of Fame in 1945.*

when Shore came from behind Bailey and hit him hard. Bailey went flying through the air and landed square on the top of his head. He writhed uncontrollably for a few minutes, then the color left his face, and all movement ceased. The players had gathered around by this time, and Bailey appeared to be dead on the ice. By this time, Shore had found himself lagging behind the others, holding up the boards toward the goal line. Red Horner headed for the dazed Eddie, and lambasted him clean on the chin, sending Shore cleanly to the ground. Blood poured from Shore's head as he was carried from the ice.

Neither Bailey nor Shore died that night, but Bailey lost his livelihood and Shore lost considerable respect. The remainder of the game was a bust. Conn Smythe assaulted a fan, causing stitches and a lawsuit, and the Leaf team spent the last of the game taking revenge on the Boston players. The final score was Toronto 4, Boston 1, and professional ice hockey 0.

On 14 February of the following year, the first all-star game was held. The players, encouraged by league president Frank Calder, pulled together an all-star team to play the Maple Leafs at Maple Leaf Gardens. All proceeds were to go to Ace Bailey, whose career had been cut short, and whose life had hung in the balance for weeks. To bring Eddie Shore to the attention of Ace Bailey may seem to have been a rather heartless and dim thing to do. Ace

TOP: *The first NHL all-star team played the Toronto Maple Leafs in Maple Leaf Gardens.*
ABOVE: *The Maple Leaf team that played the benefit game for Ace*

Bailey in 1931.
RIGHT: *Howie Morenz of the Montreal Canadiens died in the hospital after suffering a broken leg in a game.*

showed himself to be a remarkable sportsman, and Shore showed himself to be a good learner; he came to center ice wearing a leather helmet – not a bad idea for a defenseman. The two shook hands, and as the game was played the fans at the game also showed themselves to be good sports: Shore's every move was cheered by the enthusiastic crowd of well-wishers.

The game was won by the Maple Leafs, approximately $23,000 was raised, and the dream of the all-star game became a reality.

The Morenz game

The idea for the all-star game didn't exactly catch on like hotcakes, but neither did it die out entirely, for on 2 November 1937, another benefit all-star game was held, this time in the Montreal forum, on the occasion of the death of hockey's first superstar, Howie 'the Stratford Streak' Morenz.

Morenz was making his comeback in Montreal after a brief flirtation with Chicago and New York. It is very likely that

LEFT: *The 1947 NHL all-star team beat the Toronto Maple Leafs 4-3. From this year on the all-star game became an annual event.*
BELOW LEFT: *The 1937 Howie Morenz benefit game raised $25,000 for the Morenz family.*

RIGHT: *Howie Morenz in a Montreal hospital shortly before his death.*
BOTTOM RIGHT: *Albert 'Babe' Siebert captained the Canadiens in 1939.*

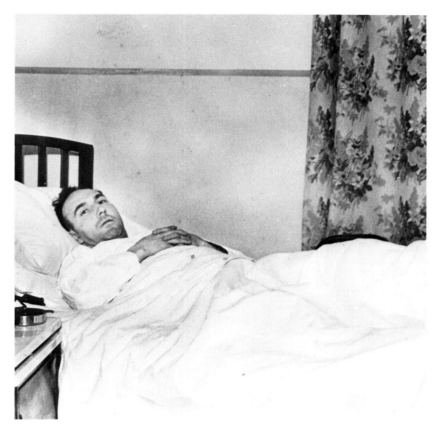

1937 would have been Morenz's last season, but he was still putting on the show Canadiens fans loved to see. The glorious Canadiens were fighting a valiant battle for first place in their division, and the Stratford Streak was leading the attack.

On the night of 28 January (the same night that Eddie Shore's career was suspended by a serious spinal injury) the Canadiens were in a furious match with the Chicago Black Hawks. Morenz had zeroed in on the Chicago net, and was at full tilt in the Hawks' zone when a frustrated Earl Siebert, the large defenseman, dove headlong at the tail of the Mitchell Meteor. Morenz's skate blade lodged in the grain of the end board only to be dislodged by Siebert's full weight seconds later. The result was multiple fractures to one of Morenz's thoroughbred legs.

Howie Morenz died rather mysteriously a few weeks later. It has often been said that Morenz died of a broken heart because he couldn't face a future without hockey. But the old-timers tell of late nights in the jovial Howie's hospital room, cheering him up with card games and his favorite vices. The story goes that he caught a virus and did not have the strength or will to fight it.

Morenz was a folk hero to the vast population of hockey fans, and a well-respected and liked man among the players. On 2 November 1937, a second all-star match was held for the benefit of the Morenz family. The Canadiens and the Maroons would combine to stand off an all-star team comprised of the greatest icemen of the time. Normie Smith of the Red Wings, Tiny Thompson of the Bruins, Toronto's Red Horner, Charlie Conacher and Busher Jackson, Johnny Gottselig and Mush March of the Black Hawks, and a variety of other household names of the time, were managed by Jack Adams to face off against the Montrealers. The all-star team won the game 6-5, and in the process raised around $25,000 for the Morenz family.

The Albert 'Babe' Siebert Game

Babe Siebert was a hardworking, rough and ready hockey player who served the game for 12 years between 1927 and 1939. He opened his career as a forward with the Maroons, and was later used as a defenseman, owing to his strength and his use of the penalty box as a tool of the trade. He put in his time with the Rangers, the Boston Bruins, and the Montreal Canadiens, and gained the respect and friendship of competitors and teammates alike.

Siebert captained the Canadiens in the 1939 season, and was chosen to coach the team the following season. In a freak accident, the Babe drowned in Lake Huron, leaving behind a great many friends and family.

The Montreal club, always known to be as classy an act in the front office as they are on the ice, hosted an all-star game for the benefit of the Siebert family on 29 October 1939. His former teammates would play against a remarkable all-star team at the forum in Montreal. The game raised approximately $15,000, and the writing was on the wall: all-star games were an attraction. By 1947 the all-star game would become an annual event whose format would change from time to time, but the notion of goodwill has remained even to the current year. Much of the proceeds of all-star games are still given to charity.

Great Forwards of the Twenties and Thirties

The twenties and thirties were great hockey days for fast skating, highly skilled stickhandling and precision goal scoring. It would be impossible to do justice to all the great forwards of this era, but there are some men who cannot be forgotten, and others who, though their names are not household words, ought to be looked at in a history of the game.

Charles William Conacher

Charlie Conacher played the majority of his 12 years with the Toronto Maple Leafs, and of his nine years with that club, he had five superlative seasons. He was five years an all-star, five times the league goal-scoring champion, twice achieved the league title for point scoring, and did regular duty as the right winger for the 'kid line' of Busher Jackson, Joe Primo and Conacher.

When he came up into the pro league in 1929/30, he scored a goal in his rookie game, in his second year led the league in points, and was instrumental in the Leaf Cup win. In 1932 he scored five times in a game against the Americans, who had Roy Worters between the pipes.

Charlie was the younger brother of Lionel, and on more than one occasion made the mistake of thinking that 'the big train' might spare him a thought. Lionel was not a dirty player, but thought nothing of teaching his kid brother a thing or two

about pain. Charlie went on to play for Detroit and the New York Americans before retiring in 1941, and was made a Hall of Famer in 1961, although his brother was never awarded this honor.

Frank Boucher

Frank was one of the great Boucher brothers of Ottawa ice hockey fame, and was without doubt the 'Gentleman Jim' of the family. His hometown team gave him his first pro contract in 1921, but after the season sent him to play in the PCHA for Vancouver. It was probably here that he learned his good manners, playing with the great Mickey MacKay for five years. He learned to be a good defensive forward, and to do it without compromising his clean, but very sharp play. When a pass was as good as a confrontation, he passed, and in his 14 seasons of professional play, earned only 118 minutes of penalty time.

With the Rangers, he played on the Cook-Boucher-Cook line, a combination that did remarkably well. He was chosen for four all-star teams, took home a pair of Stanley Cup rings, and won the Lady Byng Trophy (awarded for skill and gentlemanly play) seven times in eight years. He was so clearly identified with the Lady Byng that in 1936, they gave it to him for keeps, and Lady Evelyn Byng had another one made up!

LEFT: *The 'Kid Line' of Charlie Conacher, Joe Primeau and Harvey Jackson spent seven seasons together and amassed 792 points in regular season play, with an additional 71 points in playoff games for a total of 863 points. The line broke up when Joe Primeau decided to retire in 1936.*

RIGHT: *Charlie Conacher played right wing for Toronto and led the league in scoring for five years. He posted 31 goals in 1930/31, 34 in 1931/32, 32 in 1933/34, 36 in 1934/35 and 23 in 1935/36.*

Charles Joseph Sylvanus (Syl) Apps

Syl Apps was one of the surprising number of ice men to go on into politics. In 1940 he ran as a conservative candidate for a federal seat, but was defeated, and in 1963 was an elected provincial member for Kingston, Ontario, and made a name in the cabinet there. He was an all-round good athlete who excelled at football, pole vaulting and track events.

Apps played his entire hockey career with the Toronto Maple Leafs, joining up in 1937, when he won the first Calder Cup (Rookie of the Year) and played in Toronto until he retired in 1948. Apps was a consistent goal scorer, and stayed clear of avoidable penalties. He was aware of his value on the ice, and was a great playmaker. As captain of the team, he won three Stanley Cups, scored over 200 goals, was appointed to five consecutive all-star teams, and maintained the respect of his peers both off the ice and on.

Aubrey Victor (Dit) Clapper

This great Hall of Famer played 20 years with the Boston Bruins, from 1927 to 1947. Unlike many of his colleagues in the Hall of Fame, he did not have a remarkable first year, but worked up to star status over a couple of seasons. He was a fast and well positioned right winger, who at 6 feet 2 inches and 195 pounds, served defensive positions very capably when called upon to do so. Clapper wore number 5 for the Bruins, and the number was retired following his retirement, except for a brief stint during which Guy Lapointe was mistakenly assigned the Bears number 5.

During his time with the Bruins, Clapper three times took home Stanley Cup rings, and played on six championship teams. Although he dominated much of the Boston history for his 20 years, he is best remembered for his work with Cooney Weiland and Dutch Gainor on the 'dynamite' line. In 1930 this line lost only five games of the 44 game schedule, but was defeated by Morenz, Joliat and company in the playoffs.

Clapper coached the Bears from 1945 to 1949, and in all four years they reached Stanley Cup play. In 1947, the year he retired from active play, Clapper was elected to the Hockey Hall of Fame.

Aurel Joliat

Rearranging faces is one of the side effects of hockey, but when the star of the Montreal Canadiens, Newsy Lalonde, was traded to Saskatoon for some upstart left winger, manager Leo Dandurand must surely have put Lalonde's ample nose out of joint. Dandurand knew what he was doing, though, and the upstart Joliat proved to be just the catalyst required.

Joliat was a great crowd pleaser throughout his life. When he broke in in 1923, he took Lalonde's place on the line with Odie Cleghorn and Billy Boucher, but when in 1924 Dandurand brought the great Howie Morenz up from his Stratford

BELOW: *Dit Clapper, seen here with Eddie Shore, was part of the 'Dynamite Trio' of Cooney Weiland, Dutch Gainor and Dit Clapper.*

backwater, Joliat played on one of the most popular lines the game has ever known. In 1931 all-star teams were chosen for the first time, and Joliat was appointed along with Morenz, Bill Cook and Lester Patrick (coach) of the Rangers, Charlie Gardiner of the Black Hawks, Boston's Eddie Shore, and King Clancy, who was with Toronto at the time.

Even as a referee, Aurel was loved by hockey fans. In 1942, when he skated onto the forum ice in the uncharacteristic stripes, he received standing ovations, and the support of the crowd for his calls.

After his retirement, Joliat went on pleasing crowds with his charming personality and his gentlemanly ways. His scrapbook in the Hall of Fame contains many invitations and salutations from the prime minister of Canada, the governor general and from Queen Elizabeth herself. He proved himself to be a great entertainer on radio, television and even the cinema, where he starred in a documentary 'Les Canadiens,' made for the Canadian Broadcasting System in 1985.

LEFT: *Aurel Joliat played 16 seasons with Montreal and was known for his backhand shot.*

ABOVE: *Howie Morenz, known as 'The Stratford Streak,' played center for the Canadiens.*

Howarth (Howie) Morenz

In 1923 Leo Dandurand received a letter from Howarth Morenz, which stated that although he had signed a contract to start playing the following season, he was very sorry, but he could not come to Montreal, and hoped that Mr Dandurand would understand. Leo did not understand. He sent a train ticket and money by telegraph to Stratford asking Morenz to be in his office in Montreal at the earliest possible moment.

When Morenz arrived at the appointed place he explained to Dandurand, after much shuffling of feet and stammering, that he felt he was not good enough to become a professional hockey player with a team such as the Montreal Canadiens. Dandurand was a pretty shrewd businessman, and had a very humane approach to personnel management. On this occasion though, he demanded (with a straight face) that Morenz report to training camp or face a lawsuit. He knew full well that this kid would bend to this seemingly unkind coaxing. The rest, as they say, is history.

The Stratford Streak went on to become one of the very biggest names in the game, and played a brilliant 14-year career, most of it under Dandurand's close attention. He was the Most Valuable Player in 1928, 1931 and 1923, led in scoring in 1928 and 1931, and was the proud owner of three Stanley Cup rings.

Morenz loved to play the horses, apparently feeling an affinity for the thoroughbred beasts; he had been compared to the great pacers himself on more than a few occasions. The story is told that one night after a particularly heavy loss at the card table, he dropped a silver 50-cent piece to the sidewalk with a casual thoughtfulness. When his companion asked what the devil he was doing, he said that in the morning, some youngster would find the coin, and start off his day with a little luck. As a player of the horses, and a goal-scoring champion, he knew the value of a lucky streak.

Morenz's untimely injury and subsequent early demise is one of the great tragedies of the game. He was laid out at the Forum, where thousands jammed in to pay their respects, and even more lined the corridor of his burial procession through the streets of Montreal. His grief-stricken family was the beneficiary of an all-star game played in his honor, and the legend of Howie Morenz, the Mitchell Meteor, lives even to this day.

Great Defensemen of the Twenties and Thirties

Frank (King) Clancy

King Clancy, at 5 feet 7 inches, was one of the smaller defence-men of the period. During most of his career he weighed in be-tween 150 and 160 pounds, but never let his size influence the gusto with which he played the game. Clancy broke into the pros with the Ottawa Senators in 1922, but saw very little ice time for his first two years. Ottawa's Dey's Rink was renowned for its stingy heating system, and players like Clancy, who warmed the bench for most of the game, would have been very little use when called upon, because their feet were near frozen. Consequently, the team management rigged up a buzzer from the coaches' bench to the heated dressing room, where Clancy would cool his heels and warm his toes while waiting for the buzzer. When in 1924 he was more of a regular on the team, he was called up to play for a team he had hardly ever seen play!

Clancy was with the great Ottawa Cup-winning lineup of 1927, and was a popular man with the local fans. With the re-tirement of such well-loved icemen as Cy Denneny, Punch Broadbent and Frank Nighbor, Ottawa was very lucky to have a Frank Clancy to keep the fans coming to the rink.

Meanwhile, in Toronto, Conn Smythe was on the lookout for outstanding young players with which to rebuild his newly acquired Maple Leafs. Clancy must surely have caught the im-agination of Smythe, for in 1930, Smythe paid the record-breaking price of 35,000 dollars for Clancy, and gave two other players in the bargain. Clancy virtually led the Leafs from the beginning of his tenure with the club, and by 1932, they were hot on the trail of the Stanley Cup.

When after the 1937 season Clancy retired, he went on to his second of many careers in the hockey world. He was short-lived as coach of the Maroons, but went on to manage the team for a while, and went from there to work for the league as a re-feree. Seeing a way to make the game a lot of fun again, Clancy went back to the Maple Leafs as 'goodwill ambassador,' where until November of 1986, he could still be found advising players, coaches and the team's present owner, Harold Bal-lard. On 10 November 1986 this rare jewel went to the big rink in the sky to raise the devil with his former mates.

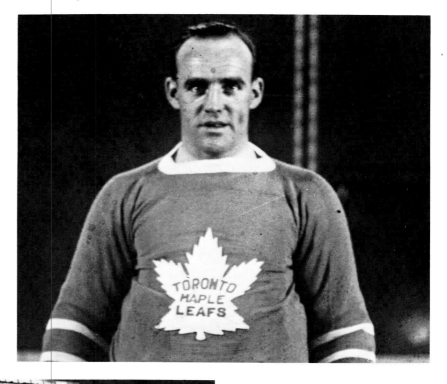

ABOVE: *Frank 'King' Clancy played for 16 years and appeared in 593 regular season games, scoring 137 goals and 143 assists. He remained active in hockey until his death in November of 1986.*

LEFT: *The Stanley Cup champion Toronto Maple Leafs of 1931/32, coached by Dick Irvin, beat the New York Rangers 3 games to 0.* RIGHT: *Lionel Hitchman, captain of the Boston Bruins, helped his team win the Stanley Cup in 1930.*

Lionel Hitchman

Hitchman is another of the many great defencemen who got his start with the Ottawa Senators. As a substitute defenceman in his first year, he probably spent many games playing cards in the dressing room with Clancy, while Eddie Gerard and George Boucher held up the regular defence duties on the ice.

In 1925 Art Ross brought him to Boston, where he played the balance of his games, most notably alongside the infamous Eddie Shore. While Shore would be rushing with the forward line, it was Hitchman who held off the opposition in the defensive zone. He played for a time with Sprague Cleghorn, who had cost Hitchman a number of teeth while with the Ottawa team. Largely due to Hitchman's clean play, Boston became a team to be reckoned with. They led the league five years out of six, and in 1930 they won 38 of their 44-game schedule, while Hitchman played 39 of those games.

During his career, Lionel Hitchman played 413 games, scored 28 goals, and spent only 393 minutes in the penalty box. Although he was one of the outstanding players of the time, he is not a member of the Hockey Hall of Fame.

Eddie Shore

This bad boy of the Boston defence probably has more stories attached to his name than any other player in the history of the game. Most of the stories are not flattering, unless one has a soft spot for bullies. Whatever his misdeeds, though, Shore was a master of the game. Most agree that he was the best defenceman of his time, and some rank him above the great Bobby Orr.

His style of play was rough, to understate the case, and he was not about to leave the scoring glory to the forwards. In his career, he scored 123 goals, and had 178 assists, for a point total of 301. His penalty record, in his day, was topped only by Red Horner. Shore served 1037 minutes; not in the same league as today's achievers, admittedly, but for the time when he was out bashing and gashing, 1037 minutes was the mark of a man to steer clear of.

Shore never won the Lady Byng Trophy, but he did win the Hart four times, was appointed to eight all-star teams, and is a member of the Hockey Hall of Fame. In 1940 he acquired the Springfield minor-league franchise, and was playing coach to a number of future stars.

RIGHT: *Cy Wentworth scored three goals and two assists in the playoffs while helping the Montreal Maroons win the Stanley Cup in 1935.*

BELOW RIGHT: *Red Dutton and Eddie Shore seen here with the Springfield Americans in 1940, a minor-league affiliate of the New York Americans. Eddie Shore acted as a player-coach at this point in his career.*

Marvin (Cy) Wentworth

This middle-weight defenceman was not a flashy player, but he was class on the glass. He broke into the pros with the Black Hawks in 1928, and partnered with Taffy Abel. In 1933 he went to the Maroons, where he remained until the end of this franchise in 1938. In 1935, when the Maroons won the Cup, Wentworth was brilliant. He played all seven games of the series, and was the playoff star of the Montreal team. Faced with such rough and tumble defensemen as Red Horner and King Clancy, he scored three goals, had two assists, and did all this without receiving any penalties!

Wentworth could have been a model for today's Soviet teams, as he was almost never out of position, was an economical checker, and drew very few needless penalties. This type of hockey interested the management of the Canadiens, and they took him on for his final two seasons. Wentworth performed very well for the Canadiens, but never repeated his wonders of the 1935 playoffs. Although he was not the type player who called much attention to himself, this stickman was just the type a netminder wants in his sights; a solid, stalwart defenseman.

Lionel Pretoria Conacher

The Big Train, as he was called, was one of the most well-rounded and colorful players in the history of the game. It is said that hockey was not his best sport, but he was a great hockey player. As a defenseman, he played 12 years and scored 80 goals, which was well over the average for the time. In 1933/34 he played with Chicago, and they won the Cup. The following year, he was with the Maroons, and alongside Wentworth, won the prize silverware again. This does not say that he made the difference, but it does say he was no slouch.

In 1924, after making a big name for himself in Canada as a football player of extraordinary talent, and a lacrosse player without peer, he went to Pittsburgh to study, and to play American-rules football. While there, he organized an amateur hockey team, the Yellow Jackets, who became a favorite with the local fans. When in 1925 the city won a NHL franchise, the Yellow Jackets were invited to join the pro ranks, and Conacher's boys became the Pittsburgh Pirates. Conacher must have known something about picking sportsmen, for the first year of entry into the league, the Pirates went to Stanley Cup play.

Conacher played around the league, working hard most of the time, and doing pretty well in the points department, and finished up with the Maroons in 1938.

Lionel Conacher was named the Canadian Athlete of the Half Century in 1950, after having achieved remarkable feats in every sport to which he turned his hand. At one point in his career, he was Canadian light-heavyweight champion, and went three rounds with Jack Dempsey. He was a member of provincial parliament, and was a liberal parliamentarian at the federal level.

Clarence (Happy) Day

Happy Day played all but his last year with the Toronto Maple Leafs, and did nearly every job in hockey but drive the Zamboni. He was a stern, hardworking leader of men who after two years at left wing, was moved behind the line, and was made captain of the team. Having studied pharmacy at the University of Toronto before entering professional hockey, he was slightly older than most of the boys, and they respected his education, thus he was both a natural and an obvious leader of men.

He was lucky enough to play behind the 'kid' line of Joe Primeau, Busher Jackson and Charlie Conacher, and the line of Baldy Cotton, Ace Bailey and Andy Blair. After 13 years with the Leafs, he went to the Americans for one final fling, where he proved a regular, but not spectacular player. After his stint with the Americans, he worked for the league in the capacity of referee, and was called back to the Maple Leafs where he coached for 10 years. In those 10 years, the Leafs won five Stanley Cups (three consecutively), and was the team to beat in every other. In 1950 he took on the front office job as manager of the team, where he remained until 1957, when he retired into business life.

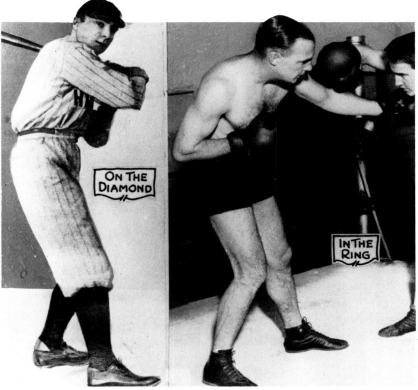

FAR LEFT: *Lionel Conacher once held the amateur heavyweight boxing championship of Canada, starred in baseball and was one of the best soccer players on the Toronto Club of the International League.*
ABOVE: *Conacher is sparring with Henry Foster, a middleweight.*

LEFT: *Conacher with the New York Americans.*

Great Goaltenders of the Middle Years

The role of the goaltender during this period had changes. The equipment changes had made the goalie somewhat more daring in his defense of the web, and had given him more prominence on the ice. Some great men took to the job, and more and more, the expertise of the goalie determined the outcome of the games.

Frank Brimsek

Francis Charles Brimsek was one of the first American-born professional ice hockey players ever to make the Hall of Fame. He was born in Eveleth, Minnesota, in 1915, and broke into hockey with the Boston Bruins in 1939. His first year may have been his best, for in this year, he won his first of two Vezina trophies, won the outstanding rookie (Calder Trophy) award, was on the first all-star team, had 10 shutouts in 44 games, a 1.58 goals-against average, and won the Stanley Cup. This would be a very difficult year to top, and although Brimsek had a great future between the pipes, his meteoric entry remained his best.

That is not to say that his later years were not bright; during his career he won another Vezina Trophy, and played on eight all-star teams. After his career was interrupted by the war, in which he served with the US Coast Guard, he returned to the rink and turned in very respectable performances until his retirement in 1950.

Charles Gardiner

Charles Gardiner is not a household name. He may, however, have been one of the best goalies of modern times. Born in Scotland, he broke into pro hockey at age 23, as the regular goalie with the lowly Chicago Black Hawks, in 1928. In his seven years he took home two Vezina trophies, played on four all-star teams, and registered a 2.13 goals-against average with 42 shutouts – all this with a team that finished last in the division for half of his career. One only wonders what he might have done with a team of winners in his corner.

Old-timers remember Gardiner with fervor. They tell of 'the guy who was the best I ever saw ….' Tragedy struck when Gardiner died at the height of his career – and the peak of his performance – of a brain tumor, at age 30.

BELOW: *Frank Brimsek played goal for the Bruins for 11 years and won the Vezina Trophy, Calder Cup and Stanley Cup in his rookie year.*
RIGHT: *Charlie Gardiner would play seven years and register 42 shutouts.*

Lorne Chabot

Lorne Chabot, at 6 feet 1 inch, was a giant among goalies. Goalies of the time tended to be rather smaller men, but Chabot's size caused him no problem in the crease. He came up into the league with the New York Rangers, under the tutelage of Lester Patrick, and played his first season so well that he replaced Hal Winkler as the regular goaltender in 1928, in his second year. Although the Rangers won the Cup, and Chabot had performed well, he had been hit by a puck above the eyes, and either Patrick sensed trouble ahead due to his injury, or he resented Chabot's hotheadedness (Chabot once was suspended for one game after punching a goal judge whom he thought needed spectacles). In any case, he was traded to the Toronto Maple Leafs for John Ross Roach and Butch Keeling.

Chabot worked hard for the Leafs, and in 1932, was able to show the Rangers that he had life in him yet, leading the Leafs to a victory and Stanley Cup in a battle with the Rangers.

Chabot played in both of the long overtime games of the thirties, winning the 1933 game between Toronto and Boston, 1-0, after 104 minutes and 46 seconds of overtime play, and losing the longer match between the Maroons and Detroit in 1936 on a fluke goal by rookie Mud Bruneteau, after 116 minutes of overtime.

In 1935 Chabot went to Chicago where he replaced the late Charlie Gardiner, and turned in a 1.83 goals-against average, won the Vezina Trophy, and was chosen for the first all-star team.

After 10 years, Lorne Chabot had a 2.12 average, two Stanley Cup rings, a Vezina Trophy and the respect of a number of managers who had written him off too early. Although Chabot is regarded as one of the outstanding players of his day, he is not a member of the Hockey Hall of Fame.

Alex Connell

Alex Connell was not known to have been a hothead, but on the one occasion when his anger did get the best of him, he found himself being pursued by an angry and powerful mobster in New York City. The game was between the Detroit Falcons and the Americans, and the betting was said to have been heavy against Detroit. The owner of the Amerks at the time was big Bill Dwyer, known by some as the King of Bootleggers, and boss of one of New York's biggest mobs. With the score tied at one in the third, Connell stopped a very close shot, and was amazed that the goal judge blazed the bulb on what was close, but clearly not in the net. Referee George Mallinson would not allow the goal, but the goal judge put up such a fracas that the game was in delay. At one point in the meeting of minds, Connell struck out at the errant goal judge and left him bleeding on the far side of the mesh. What Connell didn't know was that Dwyer, who had considerable money on the game, had fixed his right-hand man with a job in a critical spot. You guessed it. Connell was escorted by the NYPD riot squad, guns brandished, until he left town with the team on the following day.

During his career Connell won two Cups, played 12 years and retired with a 2.01 average. In 1926 he turned in a 1.2 average, and shut out 15 of his 36 games. Two years later, he recorded six consecutive shutouts (461 minutes 29 seconds). The closest anyone has come to this record is Roy Worters, when in 1931, he shut out four consecutive opponents for 324 minutes 40 seconds. Alex Connell is a member of the Hockey Hall of Fame.

LEFT: *Alex Connell played goal for Ottawa.*

ABOVE: *Lorne Chabot played with the Toronto Maple Leafs from 1928 to 1935.*

George Hainsworth

Newsy Lalonde had a reputation for picking winners. When George Vezina's untimely death shocked friends and fans, Lalonde suggested a goalie he had known in Saskatoon, Saskatchewan. This goalie was George Hainsworth, a giant of a man at 5 feet 6 inches and 150 pounds.

Lalonde's reputation was kept intact as Hainsworth won the first three Vezina Cup Awards in his first three years between Vezina's old pipes. In 1929 he played 44 games, shut out 22 opponents and turned in a 0.98 average. He won Cups in 1930 and 1931, and in 1933 had a bad year and was traded to Toronto. Hainsworth returned to Montreal to finish his career, which shows a 2.08 average overall, and a remarkable 104 lifetime shutouts.

Sam Lopresti

Sam Lopresti was a pretty good netminder. His career in professional hockey was very short, and remarkable only in that one night in March of 1941, he became a legend by making 80 stops for Chicago in a very rough game against the Boston Bruins. Chicago lost the game anyway; Lopresti may have stopped 80 shots, but he allowed three, and his opponent allowed only two.

BELOW: *George Hainsworth succeeded the late Georges Vezina in goal for the Montreal Canadiens.*

RIGHT: *Sam Lopresti is a member of the United States Hockey Hall of Fame.*

Cecil (Tiny) Thompson

Tiny Thompson burst onto the hockey scene with the Boston Bruins in 1929. He wound up his first year with a 1.18 average, and battled for the Stanley Cup for five long games. Three of the five were shutouts, and in all, he allowed three goals.

At 5 feet 10 inches and 170 pounds, Thompson was not exactly tiny. He played an excitable game, squirming and flailing around the ice. Throughout his career he did very well in the average department, but one has to allow for a remarkable pair of defencemen clearing the puck: for much of Thompson's time in the nets, Lionel Hitchman and Eddie Shore put up a stalwart defence.

In 1933 Thompson was between the posts in that memorable game between the Bruins and Toronto, which went 104 minutes overtime. Both goaltenders (Chabot was the other) put up valiant efforts, and it was inevitable that one had to give up that first goal. The Maple Leafs and Chabot won the game, 1-0, on a goal by Ken Doraty.

BELOW: *Tiny Thompson, seen here in 1929, won the Vezina Trophy four times while* *playing for the Boston Bruins, and was elected to the Hall of Fame in 1959.*

Movers and Shakers

James Norris

James Norris was a very big man in financial circles. As well as being a hockey mogul, he was owner and proprietor of the enormous grain concern, 'James Norris of Chicago,' a director of some of America's largest corporate interests, including the First National Bank of Chicago, the Chicago Rock Island and Pacific Railroad Company, Upper Lakes and St Lawrence Transportation Co Limited, Atlantic Mutual Insurance Company, the West Indies Sugar Company and Toronto Elevators Company Ltd, to name a few.

Norris was born in Montreal in 1879, and was educated at McGill University, where he contracted hockey fever, from which he never recovered. As a young man in 1907, he went west to Chicago, and began organizing the empires for which he is remembered today. When his attempts at gaining a franchise for a team in Chicago failed, he turned his interests to the Detroit Olympia, where he gained control of the then Falcons, and promptly renamed them the Red Wings.

The National Hockey League was very fortunate to have a governor of Norris' shrewd insight, devotion to the sport and money. During the Depression, times were hard for rival NHL teams, and Norris took this opportunity to expand his interest in the game. Money was hard to come by, a variety of clubs were at the mercy of bankers with foreclosure in their eyes, and before the dust settled, the Norris family had financial control of the Detroit Olympia and Red Wings, the Chicago Stadium and Black Hawks, and Madison Square Garden and the Rangers. He also owned the St Louis Arena and the Indianapolis Coliseum, perhaps foreseeing the day when those two cities would ice big league hockey teams.

From that day to this, the Norris family has been an influential force in the National Hockey League, and it seems that the bug he picked up in his McGill days is hereditary, as the Norris tradition continues.

Leo Dandurand

Joseph Viateur (Leo) Dandurand was one of the great sports promoters of his day, although, like Norris, he did not refrain from enterprise in other areas. Dandurand was an owner of racehorses, a major interest in the Montreal Royals of the International Baseball League, founded the Montreal Alouettes, and owned restaurants, laundries, dry cleaners, a wood products manufacturing firm and a soft drinks firm. But mostly, he was co-owner of the great Montreal Canadiens hockey club.

BELOW: *The Detroit Red Wings were originally the Victoria Cougars of the PCHA.*
RIGHT: *James Norris purchased the Detroit Falcons and renamed them the Red Wings.*
FAR RIGHT: *Leo Dandurand brought Billy Boucher to the Montreal Canadiens.*

Born in a town called Bourbonnais, Illinois in 1889, his family moved to Montreal in 1905, where he completed his education at St Mary's College. He began his enterprises in real estate, and there became fast friends with his lifelong partner, Joseph Cattarinich. In 1921 Dandurand, Cattarinich and a third partner, Leo Letourneau, purchased the Montreal Canadiens from the estate of George Kennedy for 11,000 dollars. Dandurand did everything right with his team: he invited politicians, judges and businessmen to join his board of directors, treated his players with care and thoughtful encouragement (in fact, he coached the team himself for a time), and brought the club such great players as Newsy Lalonde, Billy Boucher, Howie Morenz and Aurel Joliat. He did not give the team the reputation for being a fair, straightforward and classy organization, but he maintained this tradition, and after his 16-year proprietorship, turned over a successful, lean machine to the Canadian Arena Company for the tidy sum of 165,000 dollars.

Conn Smythe

Conn Smythe was the son of a Toronto theosophist, lecturer, writer and general intellectual force in the city. He was born 1 February 1895, and gave himself the name Conn on the event of his christening at age 7. He was educated at Upper Canada College, a private school for sons of the prominent and well-to-do, and at the University of Toronto, where he took a bachelor of science degree in 1920.

Smythe had a prominent military career, beginning as a gunner in the First World War, where he was wounded, taken prisoner for 14 months, and awarded the Military Cross. He went on to command the 30th (Sportsmen's) Battalion as a major in World War II, where he was seriously wounded. He was eventually given the rank of honorary lieutenant colonel for his efforts.

His hockey credentials are also rather remarkable. He coached the University of Toronto team for a number of years in the mid-1920s, and coached the gold medal team at the St Moritz Olympics of 1928. In 1925 and 1926, he organized the first New York Rangers team, which won the Stanley Cup, but did not share in the glory, as he was dismissed from his duties prior to the beginning of the season. In 1944 Smythe was offered the presidency of the National Hockey League, but turned down the offer due to his military commitments.

In 1927 he purchased the Toronto St Pats hockey club, and shortly changed the name to Maple Leafs. Smythe always claimed that the Maple Leaf was taken from the Canadian forces emblem, but he was always haunted by members of the East Toronto Maple Leaf hockey club whom he had seen play, and whose crest bore a remarkable resemblance to the one that graced the chests of his more famous Maple Leafs.

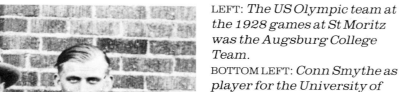

LEFT: *The US Olympic team at the 1928 games at St Moritz was the Augsburg College Team.*
BOTTOM LEFT: *Conn Smythe as a player for the University of Toronto.*
BELOW: *Conn Smythe was a guiding force in the development of the Maple Leafs.*

In 1931 Smythe built the world-famous Maple Leaf Gardens Arena in just five short months. A shortage of working capital was overcome by Smythe's shrewd ability to sell shares in the new building to workers in lieu of wages; no easy task in those bread-line days.

Smythe is also remembered for his philanthropic bent. In the early 1940s, he was approached by the Ontario Society of Crippled Children in the hopes that he would do something to aid this organization with a financial problem. They had a 50,000 dollar budget, and a deficit of nearly two-thirds that

sum. Smythe did not write a check and send them along, he headed up the finance committee for the next 20 years, building the organization to a point where their two million dollar budget covered the cost of medical assistance to every child in the province, ran seven summer camps for the disabled youngsters, and a variety of other laudable programs. He brought his Gardens such culturally significant companies as the theater Bolshoi from the USSR and the Royal Ballet from London, England. Conn Smythe, who was elected to the Hockey Hall of Fame in 1948, died in 1980, at age 85.

Frank Calder

Frank Calder never saw a hockey game until his twenty-third year. He was born at Bristol, England in 1877, and did not move to Canada until 1900. He began his career in the new world as a master of a boys' school in Montreal, and went on to be a cracker-jack sports columnist and upholder of fairness in sporting venues. With his reputation as a fine leader and spokesman, he was cajoled into taking the job as the first secretary of the National Hockey Association, and continued

LEFT: *The Conn Smythe Trophy is awarded annually to the best player in the Stanley Cup series.*

BELOW: *Frank Calder would hold the presidency of the NHL from its beginning in 1917 until his death in 1943.*

in this position until the organization evolved into the National Hockey League in 1917, when he became the first president.

Calder nursed this new league from a time when a franchise was sold for 700 dollars, to the days of the Clancy deal, when 35,000 dollars changed hands for the purchase of one player. The kind of man who wrote most of his own business letters, Calder was a stickler for detail and a diplomat of tremendous skill. It was Calder who calmed the waters during the Bailey-Shore incident, encouraging the owners and players in the staging of a benefit game, and the meeting of Bailey and Shore at center ice, showing fans, players and officials that sportsmanship was the name of the game.

Calder steered the league through many trials and near disasters, from the years when the O'Brien interests left the league with two functional clubs, to the Second World War, when hockey was able to continue only so long as it did not affect the needs of the war effort. He was not the sort to leave the work to anonymous lawyers; he had a hand and fist in every deal. Calder truly set the pace for his successors Red Dutton, Clarence Campbell and John Ziegler. His 26 years as president left a legacy of fairness, sportsmanship and goodwill that would last many years beyond his time. Frank Calder died in February 1943 in his hospital bed, with a dossier of NHL papers opened on his lap. He was truly one of the great movers and shakers of the game.

The War Years, 1939-1945

BY RALPH DINGER

It was the spring of 1939 and the hockey fans of Boston were on top of the world. Their beloved Bruins, led by slick center Bill Cowley and the ever combative Eddie Shore, had just won the Stanley Cup. However, a dark cloud soon appeared over Europe, and the hockey world would feel the effects.

During the early years of WWII the possibility that the NHL would cease operations loomed large, until on 28 September 1942, President Frank Calder issued the following statement:

> The league, now approaching its fourth wartime season, is confronted with more difficulties of operation than have been present in the three preceding years. With the institution of national selective service, it at first seemed that suspension of operations for 1942/43 must follow. However, the authorities have recognized the place which the operations of the league hold in the public interest and have, after lengthy deliberation, agreed that in the interest of public morale the league should carry on.

Calder, president of the league since its inception in 1917, would die of heart troubles less than five months later. The next 15 months would see three men, Mervyn 'Red' Dutton, Lester Patrick and E W Bickle take on the responsibilities of the presidency. Dutton, who had been a durable defenceman for over 15 big league seasons, capably handled the bulk of the duties and officially accepted the presidency on 12 May 1944.

By September of that same year, Dutton, citing private business affairs, felt he could not continue in his new role. The presidency was then offered to Major Conn Smythe. Smythe, in Europe recovering from war wounds, decided to decline.

After much persuasion, Dutton held onto the post until Clarence S Campbell accepted the presidency prior to the 1946/47 season.

This wasn't the only change that transpired in the NHL during the war years. Battles raging around the globe directly affected team fortunes, rule changes and rate of player turnover.

Nels Stewart, Red Horner, Eddie Shore, Tiny Thompson, Charlie Conacher and Harvey Jackson, celebrated stars of the past, would put away their weathered blades. This and the enlistment of more than 90 players into the armed forces necessitated the influx of many talented youngsters – many of them mere teenagers.

Elmer Lach and Maurice 'The Rocket' Richard emerged in Montreal. Chicago would gain the services of Doug Bentley and Bill Mosienko. Mosienko would have a dramatic NHL debut, scoring two goals in 21 seconds. Ironically, 10 seasons later the Winnipeg native would establish a NHL record that still stands, three goals in that same 21 seconds!

Other fresh-faced kids to enter the big-time were Ted Lindsay and Harry Lumley in Detroit. Ted Kennedy would join Toronto and make an immediate contribution. Boston also resorted to bringing in raw talent. Following their 1938/39 Stanley Cup winning season the Bruins would finish first in each of the next two seasons, culminating in another Cup win in 1940/41. Their strength was the 'Kraut' line (certainly not a popular name at this time), but before the end of the next season the three, Milt Schmidt, Woody Dumart and Bobby Bauer, were all doing their part for the allies. Needing new blood, general manager Art Ross would employ the youngest

LEFT: *The 1942 Boston Bruins would lose Nels Stewart, Red Horner, Eddie Shore, Tiny Thompson, Charley Conacher and Harvey Jackson to retirement.*
ABOVE: *Bill Mosienko holds an NHL record for scoring three goals in 21 seconds.*
RIGHT: *Elmer Lach combined with Toe Blake and Maurice Richard to form the fearsome 'Punch Line.'*

BELOW: *The 'Kraut Line' of Bobby Bauer, Milt Schmidt and Woody Dumart changed their name to the 'Kitchener Line' during WW II.*

player ever to lace up in the NHL. Still shy of his seventeenth birthday, Armand 'Bep' Guidolin began his career in the 1942/43 season. He responded admirably, scoring 22 points in 42 games. By 1944 at age 18, Guidolin would make his contribution to the war effort by enlisting in the armed forces.

Despite the absence of many players, fans flocked to arenas in large numbers. They loved the tough hockey of the day. An incident involving Wally Stanowski of the Leafs and Chicago's Dave MacKay illustrates this point. It began when young MacKay levelled Stanowski with a tremendous check along the boards. The ever colorful Leaf rearguard responded by hurling MacKay to the ice. The Hawk player was led to the dressing room with what turned out to be a separated shoulder.

While confrontations like this were going on, fans and players did not forget that there was a bigger battle going on around them. The Detroit Red Wings organization responded in spades. From the 1941/42 season until the end of the war, the Wings wore a distinctive 'V' (to symbolize victory) on their sleeves. For a time they also wore a crest that encouraged people at home to contribute in war bonds. They didn't stop there. A spine-tingling procedure had the Detroit players line up in that same symbolic 'V' pattern during the playing of the national anthems.

Fans and players would also be witness to significant rule changes during the war years. Flooding the ice surface between periods became mandatory prior to the 1940/41 season. This rule would have a dual effect. It helped to speed up the game, as players and the puck wouldn't be slowed by accumulated snow. It also reduced player injuries by removing debris from the ice.

The 10-minute overtime rule, which had been in effect since 1928/29, was now discontinued because of wartime restrictions on train travel. A regular season overtime rule would not exist again until the 1983/84 season.

The addition of the center red line for the 1943/44 season is often credited with both speeding up the game and marking the modern era in the NHL. These revelations fail to see the big picture. There is no question that the rule surrounding the introduction of the red line was an important transitionary step that helped to speed the flow of the game. However the key rule introduced affected the blue lines. Plainly said, passing the puck past one's own blue line was now permitted. This would facilitate faster breakouts and reduce the number of icing calls. Introducing the red line simultaneously, altered both of these effects. It first restricted the length of the break-out pass (actually slowing the game to a certain degree). Secondly, if the new blue line rule was instituted without the red line, a team could clear the puck once it crossed its own blue line without fear of an icing call. With the red line, icing calls would be increased (though still significantly below the standards before the new blue line rule). This could be a blessing in disguise and perhaps, is the center red line's true contribution to the game. Without the red line, a team leading in a game could continually shoot the puck into the other end once it had crossed its own blue line. This type of play would have offered little entertainment for the fans. To make a long story short, the red line did make a positive contribution to the game. However, if any credit as to speeding up the game and/or bringing the NHL into the modern era is due, the new blue line rule should be accredited.

Although the quality of play had suffered during the course of the war, star players were certainly evident. Bill Cowley, an accomplished stickhandler and playmaking center for the Boston Bruins, was a consistent point-getter.

The likes of Bryan Hextall and Lynn Patrick were bright spots for the lovers of New York hockey. An integral part of strong Ranger teams between 1939 and 1942, these two would then be witness to the unfortunate decline of this proud organization. Hardest hit by demands for manpower overseas, the New Yorkers soon found themselves the doormats of the league.

It was not a happy time for hockey in the Big Apple. The

LEFT: *Harry Lumley, Jack Adams and Ed Bruneteau in a 1944 photo wear a 'V' (the victory symbol) on their sweaters, as did the entire Red Wing team. In addition they wore crests that encouraged people to buy war bonds.*

LEFT: *Bill Cowley played center for the Bruins during WW II, and led the league in scoring in 1940/41.*
RIGHT: *The 1939/40 Stanley Cup champion New York Rangers would soon lose much of their playing strength to military service. The 1939/40 Cup win marks the last time that the Rangers won the Stanley Cup.*

New York Rangers Professional Hockey Club

LESTER PATRICK
COL. JOHN R. KILPATRICK
STANTON GRIFFIS

FRANK BOUCHER
DAVID KERR
ART COULTER CAPT.
OTT HELLER

ALEX SHIBICKY
MAC COLVILLE
NEIL COLVILLE
PHIL WATSON

Winner of THE STANLEY CUP World's Championship 1939 1940

LYNN PATRICK
CLINT SMITH
MURRAY PATRICK
BABE PRATT

BRYAN HEXTALL
KILBY MACDONALD
DUTCH HILLER
ALF PIKE
HARRY WESTERBY TRAINER

Brooklyn Americans, whose roots went back to the early days of the NHL, ceased operations following the 1941/42 season. Prior to the 1943/44 season. Rangers' managing director Lester Patrick thought along these same lines. After debating the issue, he relented and let his team play. But play they didn't. The lowly Rangers would win just six games in 50 outings!

One of the clubs that preyed on Patrick's team that year was the surging Canadiens. The 'Punch Line' of Toe Blake, Elmer Lach and Rocket Richard led the charge. Least hurt by military conscription, the Habs won 38 games during that season, then coasted to a Stanley Cup triumph. It marked their first such victory since the 1930/31 campaign, and reversed the bad times they encountered in the early days of wartime hockey.

Despite being hampered by the demands of the military, the Toronto Maple Leafs were still a consistently solid outfit throughout the war years. They never finished below third in the standings and would be the only team to claim two Cup wins in this six-year span. Their Cup victory in 1942 was particularly inspiring. After losing three straight to Detroit in the finals, the Leafs stormed back. With Syl Apps and Wally Stanowski leading the way, the Toronto club won the next four matches, snatching the silverware from the disbelieving Red Wings.

Just one year later the Wings sought and got revenge, defeating the Maple Leafs in the semi-finals. Behind the shutout goaltending of Johnny Mowers, the Wings went on to sweep past the Bruins and take the Stanley Cup.

Fan support for the Black Hawks was the biggest story in Chicago during this time. Although having a less than average hockey team, the Hawks regularly attracted large and boisterous crowds. As an example, 19,386 noisy patrons shook the rafters in historic Chicago Stadium on the night of 12 January 1941. They left with smiles on their faces as the Hawks beat the Wings that night, 2-1.

There is no question that the period between 1939 and 1945 was an extremely important growth period for the National Hockey League. The players who resumed their careers after their military responsibilities were over returned to a new game. There was a strange red line at center ice, a new man as

president of the league, six teams instead of seven and talented new players who skated fast and played hard.

When the 1945/46 season got under way, large crowds greeted their hockey heroes, both old and new. Fans showed their appreciation for the ones who fought abroad while thanking the players who did their part by keeping morale up on the homefront. All the while the hockey establishment realized the world and their game had changed for the better. This fact paved the way for the splendid years to follow.

ABOVE LEFT: Members of the 1941/42 Canadiens were least hurt by military conscription, and as a result produced strong teams during the forties.
LEFT: The 1941/42 Stanley Cup champion Toronto Maple Leafs. Conn Smythe appears in uniform and served as a major during WWII.

TOP RIGHT: Dave MacKay being helped off the ice after a collision with Wally Stanowski of the Maple Leafs.
RIGHT: Billy Taylor, Gaye Stewart, Syl Apps and Nick Metz appear in uniform in 1944.

PART III

The Golden Era 1946-1966

The Original Six

Hockey cruised through its period of greatest stability in the years following the end of World War II. Until the expansion of the NHL in 1967, big-league hockey was a six-team affair, with those teams now inaccurately referred to as the 'Original Six' playing each other 12 and then, beginning in 1949/50, 14 times a season. The NHL was comprised of the Boston Bruins, Chicago Black Hawks, Detroit Red Wings, Montreal Canadiens, New York Rangers and Toronto Maple Leafs.

It was Pullman-car hockey, with an overnight train ride being the maximum distance between NHL cities. With only six clubs, competition for NHL jobs was fierce. Gordie Howe, the Detroit Red Wings' right winger who was at the peak of his game during this era, recalls that some of the roughest play he ever saw in hockey took place not in NHL games, but in training camps when veterans and young players vied for a limited

number of spots on the big-league roster. Careers tended to be longer than they would be in the 1980s and 1990s, as players did their utmost to keep their spots in the NHL. Only 31 players in NHL history played 20 seasons in the league, and 27 of them began their careers during this era. As well, if an NHL player did get sent down to one of his club's minor-league affiliates in the American, Central, US Eastern or Western hockey leagues, he made every effort to work his way back up to the big team, even if this process took a sizeable portion of his career to complete.

With 14 games against each opposing club, rivalries were intense and players came to know one another's moves very well. This resulted in NHL hockey that placed a high premium on defense and goaltending. Defensemen concentrated on goal prevention, leaving the scoring to the forwards. Each

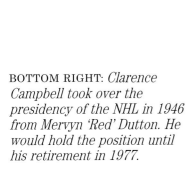

LEFT: *The Toronto Maple Leafs and Detroit Red Wings were two of the 'Original Six' teams in the NHL.*
ABOVE: *Leonard 'Red' Kelly would play a total of 20 seasons with Detroit and Toronto, and was inducted into the Hall of Fame in 1969.*
RIGHT: *Ted 'Teeder' Kennedy joined Toronto in 1942/43 and was named captain in 1948. He played 14 seasons, retiring at the end of 1956/57.*

BOTTOM RIGHT: *Clarence Campbell took over the presidency of the NHL in 1946 from Mervyn 'Red' Dutton. He would hold the position until his retirement in 1977.*

club had its number-one goalie who played almost every minute of every game.

Televised hockey began in these years that, combined with more and better reproduction of photographs in daily newspapers and magazines, delivered the images and action of the game across Canada and the United States. Players did not wear helmets, allowing for greater fan recognition. Each skater had his personality on the ice. It was a time in hockey that has provided the game with many of its greatest stars: Maurice 'Rocket' Richard, Gordie Howe, Bobby Hull, Frank Mahovlich, Andy Bathgate, Teeder Kennedy, Stan Mikita, Red Kelly, Terry Sawchuk, Glenn Hall and many others.

Competition between the clubs was fierce, but 'Original Six' hockey didn't feature parity among the fans. It was an era of dynasties, with a substantial difference in the skills level of the top and bottom clubs in the standings. For much of the era,

ABOVE: *Gordie Howe of the Red Wings chases the puck as Maple Leaf goalie Ed Chadwick attempts to clear it in a 1958 game.*

LEFT: *Terry Sawchuk holds the NHL record for most shutouts by a goaltender, with 103.*
RIGHT: *Gordie Howe, seen in 1951, would play for 32 years and score the most goals of any player in NHL history.*

Montreal, Detroit and Toronto did most of the winning. Chicago, the NHL's weakest club throughout the 1950s, became a contender in the 1960s by building an offense around two high-scoring lines featuring Bobby Hull and Stan Mikita. Of the 21 seasons from 1946/47 to 1966/67, the Canadiens, Red Wings and Leafs won 20 Stanley Cups and finished first in the regular-season standings on an equal number of occasions. The 'have-nots' appeared in the Stanley Cup finals on seven occasions, with the 1960/61 Chicago Black Hawks emerging as the only winner.

The era began with a significant event in the headquarters of the National Hockey League: Clarence Campbell accepted the job of league president, succeeding Mervyn 'Red' Dutton. Campbell, a Rhodes scholar, a soldier, a prosecutor and a former NHL referee, would hold office for 31 years and oversee the growth of the NHL from six clubs to 18.

The Dynasty Teams

The Toronto Maple Leafs, 1946-1951

Stanley Cup Champions,
1947, 1948, 1949, 1951

The Toronto Maple Leaf teams of the 1940s and early 1950s were clubs that found their stride in the Stanley Cup playoffs. On only one occasion, 1947/48, did the Leafs finish in first spot in the regular-season final standings, but for six of ten campaigns, the Leafs were Cup winners.

The Leafs were the first team in the NHL to win the Stanley Cup in three successive seasons. Their championships in 1947, 1948 and 1949 featured fine play by goaltender Turk Broda, who seemed to save his best games for the playoffs. Broda was particularly strong in goal against Detroit's superb 'Production Line' of Sid Abel, Ted Lindsay and Gordie Howe, which was the NHL's top scoring unit of the day. The Leafs and Red Wings met in the finals in 1948 and 1949, with the Maple Leafs sweeping both series four games to none. Toronto won again in 1951, this time needing five games to defeat Montreal in a series that saw every match go into overtime. During this five-year period, from 1947/48 to 1950/51, Broda's playoff goals-against average dropped each year from an already-low 2.24 in 1947 to only 1.12 in 1951.

Conn Smythe, manager of the Leafs, traded to obtain Max Bentley from Chicago in November of 1947. Bentley had been the NHL's leading scorer the previous season, playing with a Chicago team that was short on talent. Smythe traded five players to the Hawks to get Bentley, giving the Leafs another

BELOW: *Garth Boesch, Ted Kennedy, Turk Broda, Bill Barilko and Roy Conacher of the Maple Leafs defend* *their goal against Chicago.* RIGHT: *Turk Broda in 1948 with the Stanley Cup and Vezina Trophy.*

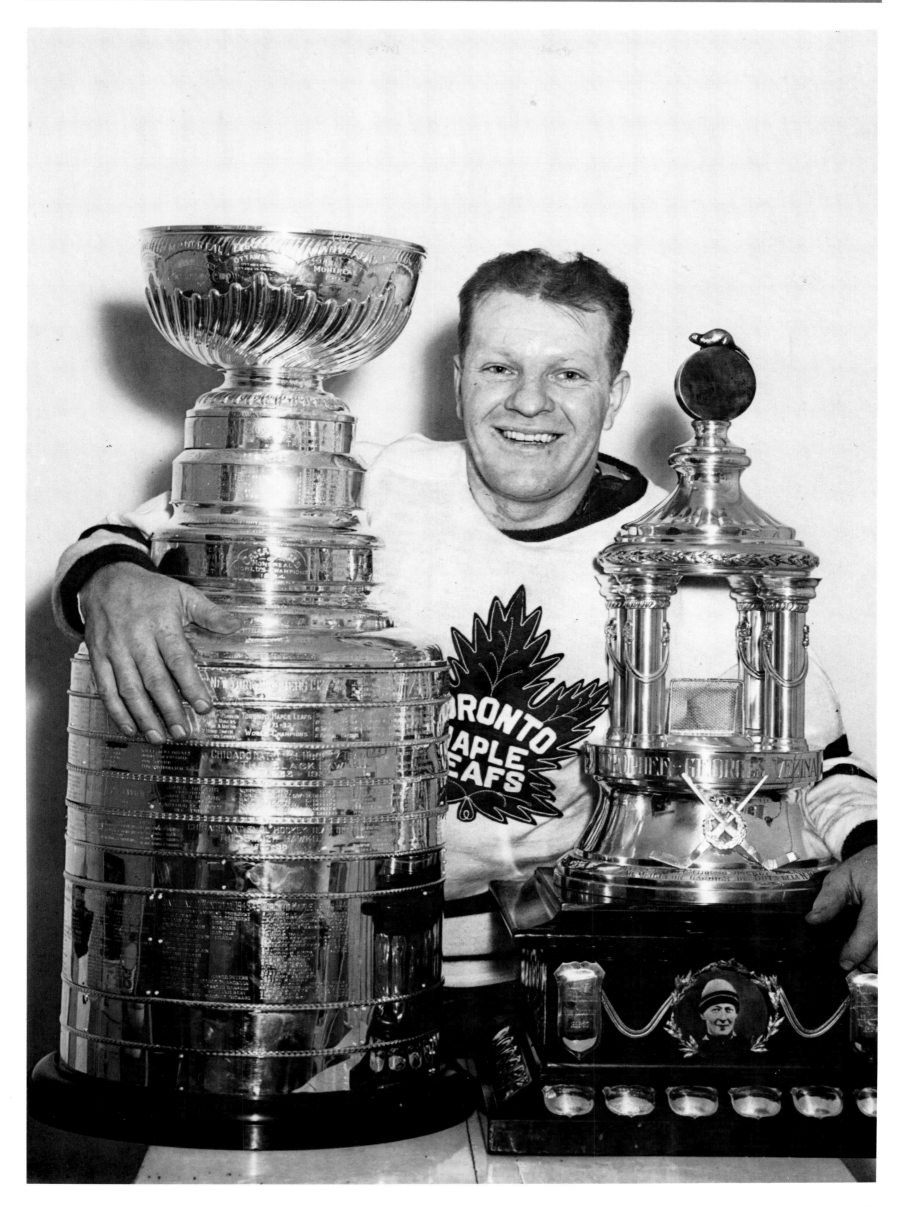

ABOVE: *Conn Smythe, Ted Kennedy and Hap Day are seen accepting the Stanley Cup from League president Clarence Campbell after their 1949 victory.*

LEFT: *Max Bentley won the Lady Byng Memorial Trophy in 1942/43, and was elected to the Hall of Fame in 1966.*

RIGHT: *Bill Barilko wins the Stanley Cup for Toronto in 1951, scoring in overtime to defeat Montreal. It would prove to be his last game, as he would die in the off-season in a plane crash.*

top centerman to go along with Teeder Kennedy, and Syl Apps who was nearing the end of his NHL career. Bentley responded to being traded to a contending team with a strong performance in the 1948 playoffs, where he registered eleven points in nine games.

Teeder Kennedy was another strong performer for the Leafs who, in the lexicon of modern hockey, would be known as a character player. He was a scrappy skater who played a tenacious style of hockey that paid off with several 20-goal seasons and a leadership role on the Leafs. When Syl Apps retired after the 1948 playoffs, Kennedy was named team captain and led the Leafs to the Cup in 1949 and 1951.

The 1951 Stanley Cup finals, which saw the Leafs defeat Montreal in their all-overtime five-game series, ended on a goal scored by Toronto defenseman Bill Barilko. Barilko was a promising young player whose greatest moment in the NHL was also his last, as he was killed in a small plane accident during the off-season.

Gus Mortson was another Leaf defenceman who was a fixture with the Toronto Maple Leafs during their Stanley Cup wins. He was tough and one of the most penalized players in the NHL, but combined these attributes with skating ability that enabled him to be an effective rusher. He was selected to the NHL all-star team in 1950. Mortson's regular defense partner was Jim Thomson, who epitomized the conservative, stay-at-home style of play. Thomson was expert at riding opposing forwards into the boards or pulling them down in front of the net. He was a two-time all-star who played 12 NHL seasons before retiring in 1958.

By the time the Leafs won the Stanley Cup in 1951, left winger Sid Smith had emerged as one of the club's top scorers. Playing on a line with Tod Sloan and Teeder Kennedy, Smith scored 30 in the regular season and seven more in the playoffs.

The Toronto Maple Leaf clubs of the late 1940s and early 1950s were unique in that they captured four Stanley Cups without having on their rosters that one dominant player who, for the period of his superiority, simply can't be stopped by opposition checkers. The Leafs were real *teams*, spreading the scoring evenly through the forward ranks and relying on great goaltending and superior defense to win low-scoring games. It was hockey molded to fit the sensibilities of manager Conn Smythe; tough, spirited and egoless.

The Detroit Red Wings, 1947-1957

Stanley Cup Champions,
1950, 1952, 1954, 1955

The Detroit Red Wings of the late 1940s had all the talent a general manager could hope for, and they had a marvelously strong young right winger named Gordie Howe. Howe simply was the complete hockey player. He rose to become not only the dominant offensive player in the NHL, but also was very likely the league's strongest, fastest, smoothest-skating and, if he felt it was required, meanest player as well. The late Charles Coleman, who compiled reports of hockey games from the 1890s to the 1960s, wrote of Howe: 'If there was anything he could not do, it has not been recorded.' What has been recorded, however, is Howe's six scoring championships, six MVP Awards and 21 all-star selections. From 1951 to 1954, when postwar NHL defense was at its zenith, Howe registered seasons of 43, 47 and 49 goals. His teammates named him 'Power' for obvious reasons. With Howe, the Red Wings finished in second place in 1947/48 and then reeled off a string of seven consecutive first-place finishes that included four Stanley Cup triumphs.

The Wings' success began when manager Jack Adams and coach Tommy Ivan put together a line of Howe on the right side, Ted Lindsay on the left and Sid Abel at center. This 'Production Line' quickly became hockey's top offensive unit and remained together for five seasons until Abel left Detroit to become the playing coach of the Chicago Black Hawks. Abel was a four-time all-star and winner of the Hart Trophy as the NHL's MVP. He was part of the Red Wings' 1950 and 1952 Stanley Cup wins and then returned to Detroit in 1957/58 as coach and, later, general manager of the Red Wings. Unlike Howe and Lindsay, who were frequently penalized, Abel committed few infractions and so played an important role as a penalty killer for Detroit.

'Terrible' Ted Lindsay was one of the toughest, most aggressive players to ever play professional hockey. Despite being only 5 feet 8 inches tall and 165 pounds, he was a feared fighter and at the time of his retirement, the most penalized

ABOVE: *The 1953/54 Detroit Red Wings.*
BELOW: *Gordie Howe would go on to hold more records* *than any other player.*
TOP RIGHT: *Left-winger Robert 'Ted' Lindsay.*
RIGHT: *Alex Delvecchio.*

player in NHL history. He combined this fiery nature with the abilities of a natural goal-scorer, a leader and a fine backchecker and defensive player. Beginning in 1948, he earned nine all-star selections in 10 years, missing only in his injury-shortened 1955 campaign. It was in this season that Lindsay recorded his best performance in the playoffs, with seven goals and 12 assists in 11 games. He was durable, scoring 379 goals in 17 NHL seasons. He remained the NHL's all-time top-scoring left winger until Bobby Hull scored his three hundred eightieth in 1967/68.

After Sid Abel's departure for Chicago, much of the centerman's work on the Production Line was done by a young player from Fort William, Ontario named Alex Delvecchio. Delvecchio was a big man and a fluid skater who could maintain the tempo dictated by Howe and Lindsay while feeding them fast, accurate passes that resulted in goals. In 1954 and 1955 – Stanley Cup-winning years for the Red Wings – the center spot on the Production Line was shared by Delvecchio, Glen Skov and Earl 'Dutch' Reibel. Delvecchio had 15 points in the Red Wings' 1955 Stanley Cup win and 10 points in 10 games in the playoffs the following season. He became captain of the Red Wings in 1962 and held this post until his retirement in 1973. At the conclusion of his career, he trailed only Gordie Howe as the NHL's all-time leader in games played, most assists and most points.

Another multiple all-star for the Detroit Red Wings was defenseman Leonard 'Red' Kelly. Kelly, along with Ted Lindsay, Gus Mortson, Frank Mahovlich and many other excellent NHL'ers, played junior hockey at St Michael's College in Toronto before joining the Red Wings in 1948. In an era in which the best skaters were usually forwards, Kelly was an exception capable of checking an opponent and rushing up the ice at top speed. He did spot duty with Detroit as a left winger and, in fact, completed his career as a center. In the early 1950s, he had an almost permanent claim on a first team all-star berth on defense, sharing this honor with Montreal's Doug Harvey. When the Norris Trophy awarded to the NHL's top defenseman was commissioned in 1954, Kelly was its initial winner. He also was a four-time winner of the Lady Byng Trophy for gentlemanly conduct. Kelly was a vital part of the Wings' four Stanley Cup wins and, unique in the postwar NHL, would prove to be an equally important component in another four-Cup hockey dynasty, that of Toronto Maple Leafs in the early 1960s.

Like all powerhouse teams, the Red Wings enjoyed spectacular goaltending – provided by Terry Sawchuk. Despite an edginess and repeated bad nerves, he played more than 20 seasons in the NHL and is the only goaltender in the league to register more than 100 shutouts. During the Red Wings' glory years, Sawchuk registered five consecutive seasons in which he allowed fewer than two goals per game. His playoff performance in 1952 is even more remarkable, as he allowed only five goals in eight games, registering four shutouts en route to the Stanley Cup.

The builder of the great Detroit clubs was general manager Jack Adams, who had been one of hockey's top players in the 1920s. Adams also coached the team from 1927 to 1947. Adams' Detroit teams made the playoffs for 20 consecutive seasons, beginning in 1938/39. He was the first to develop a comprehensive farm system to provide his NHL team with a steady supply of talent that was schooled in the kind of hockey the Red Wings played. Players like Sawchuk and Howe were signed on as Red Wings' property when they were only 13 and 14 years old. It was through Adams' system of developmental teams in cities like Omaha and Indianapolis that they arrived in the NHL with their talents and enthusiasm for the game intact.

Jack Adams relinquished his coaching responsibilities to Tommy Ivan beginning with the 1947/48 season. Ivan-coached teams finished first in six of seven seasons and won

the Stanley Cup three times in the same period. When Jim Norris, Jr, the son of the Red Wings' owner, bought the troubled Chicago Black Hawks franchise in 1954, Ivan was hired as general manager with a specific mandate to develop a Jack Adams-style farm system to make the team a contender.

The Montreal Canadiens, 1955-1960

Stanley Cup Champions,
1956, 1957, 1958, 1959, 1960

It is difficult to define precisely the beginning and end of the Montreal Canadiens' reign as the NHL's resident powerhouse. The franchise has won so frequently and moved to strengthen its hockey team so swiftly that even the gaps in the Canadiens' dominance seem, when viewed 20 or 30 years removed, to be merely a pausing for breath in a logical progression forward.

The Canadiens won the Stanley Cup five straight seasons beginning in 1955/56. After winning in 1953, only a deflected screen shot in overtime of the seventh game of the finals

against Detroit in 1954 and the suspension of their top scorer, Maurice 'Rocket' Richard, for the entire 1955 playoffs, separated the Canadiens from a possible eight consecutive Stanley Cup triumphs.

Beginning in 1955/56, coaching these powerhouse Montreal teams was entrusted to Toe Blake. Blake was a former star player with the Canadiens and right wing on the famed 'Punch Line' with Elmer Lach and Rocket Richard. Blake succeeded Dick Irvin, Sr behind the Canadien's bench and was

given the job with the understanding that one of his principle tasks was to ensure that Rocket Richard did not fall victim to his extraordinarily fiery nature. Irvin, who had coached the team from 1940 to 1955, had won the Cup three times, but in doing so, he permitted and, according to some hockey insiders of the era, encouraged Richard to give vent to his considerable temper on the ice.

The Richard Riot

The most damaging of Richard's outbursts occurred in a game against the Boston Bruins on 13 March 1955. Here is how the incident is described in the proceedings of the disciplinary hearing convened in the offices of the National Hockey League on 16 March:

Around the fourteen minute mark of the third period when Boston was a man short, the Canadian goalkeeper was removed in favor of a sixth forward. Richard skated past [Hal]Laycoe who high-sticked him on the head. Referee [Frank] Udvari signalled a penalty to Laycoe but permitted the play to continue as the Canadiens were still in possession of the puck. Richard skated around the Boston goal and almost to the blueline when the whistle blew. Richard rubbed his hand on his head and indicated to the referee that he had been injured. Suddenly he skated towards Laycoe, who had dropped his stick and gloves, and swinging his

BELOW LEFT: *Canadiens celebrate after defeating Detroit on 10 April 1956.*

BELOW: *Maurice 'The Rocket' Richard became a Montreal legend.*

[Richard's] stick up with both hands, he struck Laycoe a blow on his shoulder and face. The linesman grabbed the two players and Richard's stick was taken from him. Richard broke away from linesman [Cliff] Thompson and, picking up a loose stick, again attacked Laycoe, striking him over the back and breaking the stick. The linesman seized Richard but he got away and seizing another stick, attacked Laycoe for a third time, hitting him on the back. Linesman Thompson seized Richard once more and, forcing him to the ice, held him there until a Canadien player pushed him away and Richard gained his feet. Richard then struck Thompson two hard blows in the face which raised a swelling. Richard was finally brought under control and taken to the first aid room where several stitches were required to close a cut on the side of his head. Referee Udvari gave Richard a match penalty for deliberately injuring Laycoe and Laycoe was given a major penalty. Laycoe was ordered to take his place on the penalty bench and when he failed to do so, the referee gave him a ten-minute misconduct penalty. Laycoe claimed that he had been hit first on the glasses . . . . Richard said he thought Thompson was one of the Boston players.

NHL president Clarence Campbell attended the disciplinary hearing and concluded that Richard's attack on Laycoe was deliberate. He sited a similar incident involving Richard in a game against Toronto on 29 December 1954. He stated that Richard's 'pattern of conduct was almost identical, including his constant resort to the recovery of his stick to pursue his opponent, as well as flouting the authority of the officials. . . . At that time he was warned there must be no further incident. . . . Richard will be suspended from all games both league and playoff for the balance of the current season.'

The response of Montreal's hockey fans boiled over on 7 March when president Campbell appeared in his regular seat at the Canadiens' home game against Detroit. By the end of the evening, the Montreal Forum was evacuated in a cloud of tear gas, the game forfeited to Detroit and Ste Catherine's Street in downtown Montreal devastated by hooligans. The night's activity came to be known as the Richard Riot.

In hockey terms, the suspension cost Richard the best opportunity in his career to win the NHL scoring championship. It was a factor in the Canadiens' regular-season finish two points behind Detroit and removed the club's leading scorer and the NHL's top playoff performer from a lineup that would still get to the seventh game of the finals before elimination.

Canadiens general manager Frank Selke, Sr knew Richard had run out of chances with the NHL authorities. His choice of Blake to guide the team was inspired. Blake had the respect of Richard as well as of all the players. He spoke both English and French and, as a former star player, knew what an athlete had to do to win. It is the coming of Blake and the soothing of Richard that made the Montreal Canadiens unbeatable for five seasons in the NHL.

Maurice 'Rocket' Richard had been Montreal's most exciting player in the postwar era. As a young star, he scored 50 goals in 50 games in 1944/45, and led the NHL in goals scored in five seasons. He was plagued by serious leg injuries at the beginning and end of his career, but when he was healthy he was surely the most exciting player in the NHL. He drove straight to the net, warding off opposing checkers with one arm as he cut in on goal. Like Gordie Howe, he was ambidextrous with a strong backhand and wrist shot. Manager Selke said, 'Not only was he endowed with phenomenal strength, but the Rocket possessed an unparalleled instinct. He was the most opportunist player I have ever seen.' The Canadiens' five-year run of Stanley Cup championships coincided with the end of the Rocket's career. Though injuries kept him out of the lineup for large portions of each of his last three seasons, he still was an important force on the team, communicating his passionate need to win to all the other players on the club.

Three other Montreal Canadien forwards led the NHL in goals or points scored in the regular season during the club's five year championship reign. Bernie Geoffrion, Dickie Moore and Jean Beliveau joined the Canadiens in the early 1950s. They were all native Quebecers and born in 1931, forming perhaps the greatest one-year harvest of local talent to ever play in the NHL.

Bernie Geoffrion was the NHL's rookie-of-the-year in 1952. He was a spirited player who made up for limited skating skills by becoming a great stickhandler and the possessor of a wicked shot. His nickname, 'Boom-Boom,' came from the sound the puck made when his heavy slapshot hit the end boards and bounced back into play. Geoffrion became the second player in the NHL to record a 50-goal season, equalling Richard's mark in 1960/61. He and Jean Beliveau were members of a particularly effective line in which left winger Bert Olmstead, himself a two-time all-star, did much of the digging and corner work to get the puck out to his high-scoring linemates.

LEFT: *The aftermath of the Richard Riot in Montreal in March of 1955, caused by Richard's suspension by Clarence Campbell for fighting.*
BELOW LEFT: *Clarence Campbell, seen with handkerchief trying to ward off tear gas, was pelted with fruit and overshoes by the Montreal crowd.*

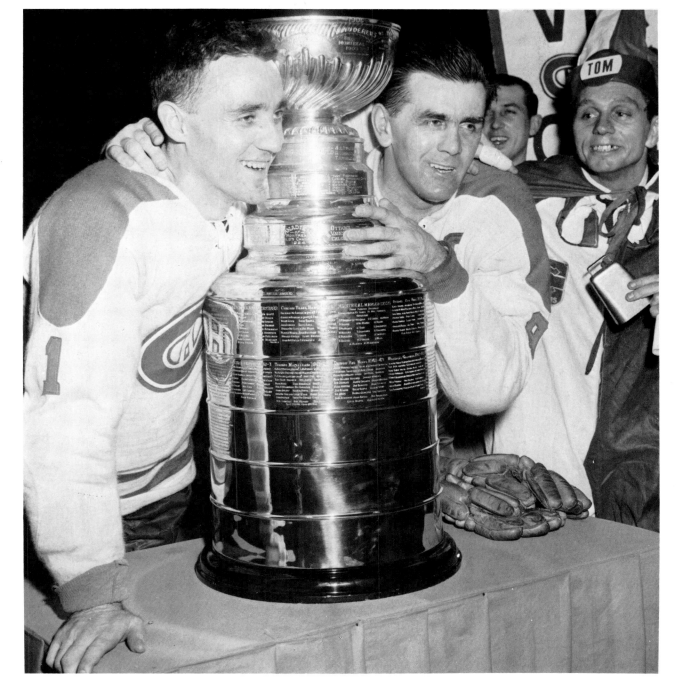

RIGHT: *Jacques Plante and Maurice Richard with the Stanley Cup in 1960. This would be Richard's last Cup victory.*

Dickie Moore set the single-season point-scoring record with 41 goals and 55 assists for 96 points in 1958/59. He was a strong skater with an aggressive streak who complemented the many linemates he had during his 12-year career in Montreal. His most productive campaigns coincided with the Canadiens' lock on the Stanley Cup.

Jean Beliveau became the most celebrated player in the Canadiens' organization, combining impressive playing skills with leadership abilities and a gentlemanly bearing that has made him one of hockey's most visible and highly-regarded spokesmen. Even his arrival on the Canadiens' roster was surrounded by special circumstances. He had enjoyed a celebrated junior and senior hockey career in Quebec City and, in brief tryouts with the Canadiens in 1951 and 1953, demonstrated that he was a top NHL-caliber player. But his situation in Quebec suited him; he was a hero and while supposedly an amateur, was said to be making a much greater salary than he could have expected to earn as a young player in the NHL. The Canadiens, desperate to add his talents to their NHL roster, purchased the entire Quebec Senior League in 1953, turned it into a professional circuit and promoted Beliveau to their NHL roster. He was instantly effective with Montreal, dominating the game. In an era of smaller players, Beliveau at 6 foot 3 inches stood out on the ice. He led the NHL in scoring in 1956/57 with 47 goals and 88 points, and added 12 goals and seven assists in the playoffs. His long career ended on a winning note in 1971, having been on 10 Cup-winners while scoring 1219 points in 18 NHL seasons.

Coach Toe Blake added two other new players to the Canadiens' roster for 1955/56 — Henri Richard and Claude Provost. Both were regulars throughout the Canadiens' five-year hold on the Stanley Cup.

BELOW: *Jean Beliveau in 1949 as a junior with the Citadelle of Quebec.*

RIGHT: *Ranger goalie Lorne Worsley makes a save against the Canadiens as players fight for the rebound.*

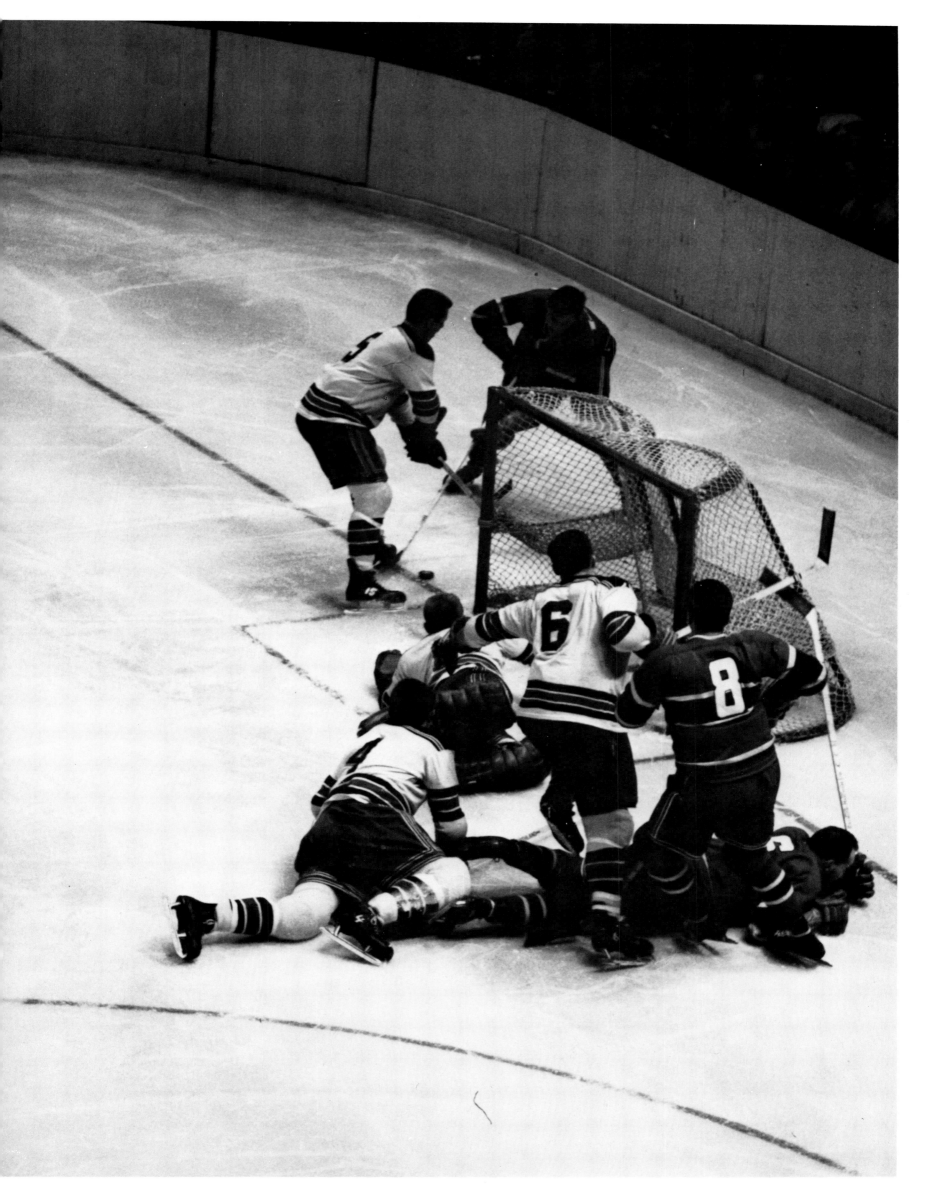

ABOVE: *Jacques Plante, in goal for Montreal with the original mask he designed, was the first goalie to regularly wear such protection.*

LEFT: *Lorne 'Gump' Worsley makes a save on Henri Richard during the 1956 playoffs.* RIGHT: *Henri Richard, the younger brother of Maurice, was nicknamed 'The Pocket Rocket.'*

Henri Richard was the younger brother of the Rocket. At only 5 feet 7 inches, he used his tremendous skating speed to evade opposing checkers. A right wing and a center, he showed both a scoring touch and an ability to set up his linemates. He had 80 points in 1957/58, second only to teammate

Dickie Moore. In the 1960 playoffs, which the Canadiens swept in the minimum eight consecutive games, Henri Richard had 12 points. He played on 11 Stanley Cup winners in 20 NHL seasons.

Claude Provost was Montreal's consummate defensive forward. Playing from the right side, he often drew the task of shadowing the top scorers on opposing teams. He was one of the NHL's best checkers, combining surprising speed with the strength required to skate a strong forward out of the play. He was at his best matched against Bobby Hull when the Chicago star emerged as one of the league's fastest and strongest men.

The Montreal defense corps during the 1950s was anchored by Doug Harvey, who was selected to the NHL all-star team for 11 consecutive years beginning in 1952. Harvey was a puck-control specialist, gaining and maintaining possession until the offense had formed up around him. Only then would he pass off to the player in the most advantageous position. He won the Norris Trophy as the NHL's outstanding defenseman on seven occasions, a record surpassed only by Bobby Orr, who won the award eight times.

Jacques Plante was the Canadiens' innovative goaltender. He is best remembered as the pioneer of the protective mask, but also widened the goalie's puck-handling responsibilities. His style of leaving his net to stop pucks shot around the end boards or to pick up the puck when it was dumped in by the opposing team has become a standard part of any goaltenders repertoire. He was a six-time all-star with a lifetime goals-against average of 2.40 in the regular season and 2.18 in the playoffs.

The Chicago Black Hawks, 1960-1967

Stanley Cup Champions, 1961

The Chicago Black Hawks were a have-not team saved from the brink of dissolution in the mid-1950s by new ownership and a commitment to rebuild in the old style. In the 12 seasons from 1946/47 to 1957/58, the Black Hawks finished sixth and last on nine occasions. Crowds in the old Chicago Stadium had dropped to below the 5000 level, as prospects for improvement were bleak. Jim Norris, Jr bought the Chicago club in 1954 and hired Tommy Ivan, the successful coach in Detroit, as his general manager and Dick Irvin, the coach of the Canadiens, as his coach. Ivan set out to build a solid farm system of sponsored junior and minor-pro clubs. The system began to bear fruit before the end of the 1950s as first Bobby Hull and then Stan Mikita graduated from the St Catherines, Ontario juniors to the Hawks. Shortly after ill health forced Dick Irvin to retire, Rudy Pilous, who had coached Hull and Mikita in St Catherines, found himself in the NHL as well. In 1960/61, the Black Hawks won the Stanley Cup, the only time between 1941 and 1969 that a team other than Montreal, Detroit or Toronto was victorious.

Bobby Hull was a dream player with movie star good looks, tremendous speed and strength and the most powerful shot in hockey. He was a two-way player, combining his offensive skills with stickhandling and checking abilities. His rising slapshot caused many NHL goaltenders to don a mask for the first time in their careers. He was the NHL's top scorer in his third NHL campaign when he was combined with Billy 'Red' Hay and Murray Balfour on what came to be called the 'Million-Dollar Line.' Equalling the NHL record of 50 goals in a single season in 1962, Hull went on to shatter this mark in 1966 with 54 goals, despite missing six games with a knee injury. One of his linemates during his record-breaking 1966

season was Phil Esposito, who would go on to be one of the NHL's top players in the late 1960s and 1970s.

Stan Mikita was a tough, little center who dug for the puck and created opportunities for his linemates. He took many unnecessary penalties in his early NHL years, but changed his style and won the Lady Byng Trophy for gentlemanly conduct twice in his career. Along with Hull, Mikita was one of the first to use a curved stick blade. This device caused the puck to dip in flight, adding to the goaltenders' problems. Hull, who was best known for his slapshot, used this characteristic of the curved stick to good advantage, but Mikita was able to enhance both his forehand and backhand shots with the curved blade. In the Hawks' Cup-winning season, Mikita became part of the 'Skooter Line' with Ken Wharram and Ab McDonald.

Chicago had the good fortune to employ the game's most durable goaltender, Glenn Hall. Hall played in 502 consecutive NHL games, was a rooke-of-the-year, and recorded 84 shutouts in the regular season. He played 18 years in the NHL and was an 11-time all-star.

Pierre Pilote was a standout defenseman for Chicago, playing most of his career with Elmer 'Moose' Vasko. Pilote would carry the puck and was the era's top-scoring defenseman. His 14 goals and 45 assists for 59 points in 1965 set a new single-season scoring record for blueliners. Pilote was selected to the NHL all-star team eight consecutive times. He won the Norris Trophy as the NHL's top defenseman on three occasions.

BELOW: *Chicago goalie Glenn Hall makes a diving save as teammate Jack* *Evans and Maple Leaf Bob Pulford skate after the rebound.*

The Toronto Maple Leafs, 1961-1967

Stanley Cup Champions,
1962, 1963, 1964, 1967

The four Stanley Cups won by the Toronto Maple Leafs during the 1960s are a tribute to the skills of coach and general manager Punch Imlach, who molded a solid group of veteran and young players into a unit that was good enough to win consistently at a time when the NHL had four strong teams – Toronto, Detroit, Montreal and Chicago. Though he drove, needled and cajoled his players, Imlach stuck by the men he believed in. When the Leafs proved incapable of winning the Stanley Cup in 1965 and 1966, fan and media pressure mounted for Imlach to make major changes and overhaul his lineup by replacing several of the veterans who had performed so well in previous seasons. Imlach held his ground, staying with his old pros, and won the 1967 Stanley Cup. The players he had on the ice at the end of regulation time averaged 38 years of age.

The Leafs were built from their defense out. Their first five defensemen – Bob Baun, Red Kelly, Tim Horton, Allan Stanley and Carl Brewer – would have been welcomed on the roster of

any other club. Bob Baun was a fine skater and solid checker. He earned a place in the lore of the sport with a remarkable display of stoicism in the sixth game of the 1964 Stanley Cup finals against Detroit. With Detroit leading 3-2 in games and game six tied at three goals a piece after regulation time, Baun, refusing to succumb to a very painful leg injury sustained earlier in the match, scored the winning goal in overtime. He played strongly in Toronto's seventh game win as well and only then, with the Stanley Cup safely in hand, did he submit to an X-ray which revealed a broken bone in his ankle.

Carl Brewer was the fastest-skating of the Leaf defenders and another player who could have done well as a forward. He was an emotional player which resulted in his being frequently penalized. Despite his considerable abilities, he and Imlach did not get along, resulting in Brewer's resignation from the team after the 1965 playoffs. He was later reinstated as an amateur and joined Canada's national amateur team.

Red Kelly, who had starred with Detroit in the early 1950s, was equally important to the Leafs in the 1960s. By 1965 he spent much of his playing time at center, but during the Leafs' first three Cups in the 1960s, he contributed from the defenseman's spot.

BELOW: *Punch Imlach would guide the Maple Leafs to four consecutive* *Cup wins in the sixties as coach and general manager.*

Tim Horton was one of those NHLers whose reputation as a strongman was so widely recognized that he was only rarely required to demonstrate his prowess as a hardrock. Horton was such a fine skater that, when injuries depleted the Toronto bench, he was occasionally used as a forward. He had an exceptional year in the 1962 playoffs, leading the Leafs in points with three goals and 13 assists.

Allan Stanley played 10 NHL seasons for New York, Boston and Chicago before a trade brought him to the Leafs. At 6 feet 2 inches, he was a big man who could rush with the puck. He earned three all-star selections during his years in Toronto.

Johnny Bower was a fine goaltender caught in the log-jam of the six-team NHL. After a strong season in the nets for New York in 1954, he spent almost all of the next five seasons in the minors before being acquired by the Leafs for the 1958/59 season. Unlike some of the other iron men who played goal in the NHL, Bower shared the goaltender's job during the regular season (Imlach made sure of this) so he would be sharp for the playoffs. His best year in the post-season was in 1963 when his goals-against average was only 1.60 in 10 playoff games. Beginning in 1965 he was part of a true two-goalie system, as Imlach had acquired Terry Sawchuk to combine with Bower and give the Leafs exceptionally experienced goaltending.

The Leafs' most exciting forward was Frank Mahovlich, a rookie-of-the-year and six-time all-star. Mahovlich set the single-season scoring mark for the Leafs with 48 goals in 1961. He had a unique, swooping skating style and, on a good night, seemed to be able to do anything he wanted with the puck. He led the Leafs in scoring for six straight years during the 1960s, but still never seemed to be giving Imlach and the Toronto fans enough. His potential was seen as so vast that Jim Norris, the owner of the Chicago Black Hawks, offered Toronto management one million dollars for Mahovlich's contract. This highly-publicized transaction never came about and, eventually, Mahovlich was traded to Detroit and Montreal, where he played some of his finest hockey.

Dave Keon joined the Leafs in 1961, centering either Mahovlich and Bob Nevin or George Armstrong and Dick Duff. He was a 20-goal scorer in his first season and won the Calder Trophy as rookie-of-the-year. Keon ranked as one of the fastest skaters in the NHL and combined this speed with clean play. In 22 big-league seasons, he spent only 117 minutes in the penalty box.

Long-time Toronto fans say they can never remember him being hit solidly by an opposing bodychecker. He was a great Stanley Cup competitor, scoring all three Toronto goals in the Leafs' seventh game win over Montreal in the 1964 semifinals, as well as winning the Conn Smythe Trophy as playoff MVP in 1967.

Another player who contributed to the Leafs' 1964 Stanley Cup was right winger Andy Bathgate. Bathgate was the brightest offensive star for the New York Rangers from the mid-1950s onward, winning the Hart Trophy as NHL MVP after a 40-goal performance in 1959. He was traded to Toronto in February of 1964. He fitted in with the Leafs' style and made an excellent linemate for Frank Mahovlich. He had nine points in the playoffs and enjoyed the only Stanley Cup win of his illustrious career.

The Montreal Canadiens, 1965-1968

Stanley Cup Champions,
1965, 1966, 1968, 1969

By the time the Canadiens re-established themselves as the NHL's best, the glorious star-laden teams of the late 1950s had given way to more workmanlike squads. Beliveau, Henri Richard and Provost were team leaders who carried over the winning tradition.

Lorne 'Gump' Worsley and Charlie Hodge gave the Canadiens capable goaltending in the last years of the six-team NHL. Worsley was acquired by the Canadiens in a trade that sent Jacques Plante to the New York Rangers. With New York, Worsley had established himself as a top goaltender who never had the benefit of a strong team in front of him. He was less temperamental than Plante, who suffered from recurring asthma and allergic reactions. As a member of the Canadiens, Worsley played on four Cup-winners, sharing the Vezina Trophy as top goaltender on two occasions. His 21-year career took him into the 1970s and saw him record a lifetime goals-against average of 2.90. He was one of the last goaltenders not to wear a mask. Charlie Hodge had backed up Plante during the late 1950s and continued the same role when the Canadiens acquired Worsley. He played regularly in 1964, after Worsley was injured early in the season, and won an all-star berth and the Vezina Trophy. He shared this award with Worsley again in 1965.

John Ferguson was a big left winger who added an important dimension of toughness to the Canadiens in the 1960s. The Montreal club was made up of a lot of smaller players who found themselves outmuscled in the tough going of the playoffs in the early 1960s. The addition of Ferguson changed that. As a 25-year-old NHL rookie, he quickly gained a reputation as a good hockey player and a ferocious fighter who would take on any opponent who menaced the smaller Canadiens' stars. This resulted in more skating room for the Canadiens' players and five Stanley Cups for Ferguson in eight NHL seasons.

Typical of these smaller skaters was Yvan Cournoyer, who joined the Canadiens in 1963/64. At 5 feet 7 inches and 178 pounds, Cournoyer had several big scoring years to come after expansion, and was another candidate for the unofficial title of 'Fastest Man in Hockey.'

The best of the Canadiens' fine defense corps was Jacques Laperriere, who won the Calder Trophy as rookie-of-the-year in 1964. At 6 feet 2 inches, he was able to use his big reach and strength to cover a lot of the rink and ride opposing players out of harm's way. He was a four-time all-star and the Norris Trophy winner as top defenseman in 1966. Serious knee injuries shortened his career.

Coach Toe Blake retired after winning the 1968 Stanley Cup, his eighth in 13 years as a coach.

LEFT: *Frank Mahovlich scores a goal against the Rangers' Marcel Paille in 1961.*

BELOW: *Lorne 'Gump' Worsley was one of the last goalies not to wear a mask.*

Champions without Championships

Many marvelous hockey players enjoyed long and successful NHL careers without the particular pleasure of playing on a Cup-winning team.

Leo Boivin entered the NHL in 1952 with the Toronto Maple Leafs. He was traded to the Bruins in 1954/55, and played 11 seasons in Boston. Boivin was a sturdy defenseman who was famous for thunderous body checks. At 5 feet 7 inches and 190 pounds, he was a tough man to move. He reached the Stanley

BELOW LEFT: *Leo Boivin played defense for Toronto and Boston and was feared for his hard bodychecking. He played for 13 seasons but never won the Stanley Cup.*

BELOW: *Bill Gadsby watches Al Rollins make a diving save on Howie Meeker's backhand shot.*

Cup finals on three occasions in a career that spanned more than 1100 games, but never played on a winner. He was inducted into the Hockey Hall of Fame in 1986.

Bill Gadsby played 20 years in the NHL, during which time he was selected to the NHL all-stars on eight occasions. He was a rushing defenseman who set up his share of goals. Along with Red Kelly, he was the highest scoring rearguard of the 'Original Six' era. He was a mainstay of the defense for Chicago, New York and Detroit. He retired after the 1965/66 season.

Camille Henry starred with the New York Rangers and was the NHL's top rookie in 1954. Henry was tall, slim and a great skater. He was a natural center and, after stints in the minors, made the team to stay in 1958. He won the Lady Byng Trophy that year, finishing with just one two-minute penalty after 70 games of action. His 32 goals that season earned him an all-star selection. He had another strong campaign in 1963, with 37 goals and 23 assists for 60 points.

ABOVE: *Camille Henry played center for the Rangers and won the Calder Cup and Lady Byng Trophy in 1954.*

RIGHT: *'Sugar' Jim Henry played goal for the Black Hawks, Rangers and Bruins but never was on a winner.*

108

'Sugar' Jim Henry played goal for Chicago and the New York Rangers before coming to Boston in 1952. The early 1950s were Boston's only bright spots in the postwar years, and Henry's strong goaltending helped the team get to the finals in 1953. The previous season Henry was victimized by Rocket Richard in what has been described as hockey's most dramatic play. Richard had been knocked out early in the seventh game of the semi-finals, and returned with the score tied 1-1 with only a few minutes to play in the third period. He skated the length of the ice with the puck, moved in on Henry and scored the winner. It later was determined that Richard didn't pass the puck because his vision was still blurry from his earlier encounter.

Bronco Horvath knocked around in the minor leagues with only occasional appearances in the National Hockey League until he was drafted by the Boston Bruins in 1958. With Boston he emerged as a high scorer, recording 30 goals in his first year with the team. He was part of the 'Uke Line' with John Bucyk and Vic Stasiuk, combining for 174 scoring points that season. In 1960 he tied with Bobby Hull as the NHL's top goal scorer, with 39, and was selected as a member of the all-star team.

Harry Howell played 24 seasons in big-league hockey, largely with the New York Rangers. He was an effortless skater and a defenseman's defenseman. He was team captain, won the Norris Trophy and was selected an all-star in 1967, his fifteenth NHL season.

Billy Mosienko played 14 seasons with the Chicago Black Hawks. He was an exceedingly fast skater and a great stick-handler who averaged less than 10 minutes in penalties per season. He was part of the 'Pony Line' with brothers Doug and Max Bentley. This trio of small, fast players led all forward combinations with 179 points in 1947. In 1952 Mosienko scored 31 goals and set an NHL record that probably is un-breakable: three goals in only 21 seconds.

BELOW: *Harry Howell played for most of his 24 seasons with the Rangers, and was inducted into the Hall of Fame in 1979.*

RIGHT: *Bill Mosienko played for Chicago for 14 years and set a record in 1952 of three goals in 21 seconds that still stands.*
BELOW RIGHT: *Brothers Doug and Max Bentley played with Bill Mosienko on the 'Pony Line' and led the league in points for a forward line in 1947.*

Bill Quackenbush was an effective rushing defenseman who played for Detroit and Boston. He was one of the NHL's best checkers, but was able to impede his opponents without drawing penalties. He went through the entire 1948/49 regular season and 11 playoff games without a penalty, becoming the first defenseman to win the Lady Byng Trophy as the league's most gentlemanly player. Quackenbush also received five all-star selections.

Norm Ullman became a regular with Detroit Red Wings just after the team slid from the top tier of NHL clubs in the late 1950s. He reached the 20-year milestone in the NHL, scoring more than 20 goals in 16 seasons. This slick center's best year was 1965, when a league-leading 42 goals earned him a spot on the all-star team. In 1967/68, he was involved in the biggest trade of the era when Ullman, Paul Henderson and Floyd Smith moved to Toronto in exchange for Frank Mahovlich, Pete Stemkowski, Gary Unger and the rights to Carl Brewer.

LEFT: *Bill Quackenbush with Milt Schmidt in 1952. Quackenbush was the first defenceman to win the Lady Byng Trophy.*

BELOW: *Norm Ullman played center for the Red Wings after the team's successful years, and was traded to Toronto.*

Fine Tuning the Rules

The addition of the center ice red line in 1943/44 was the first of many rule changes designed to speed up play and increase skating room on the ice surface. The goaltender's crease was enlarged from 3×7 feet to 4×8 feet, and the face-off circles enlarged from a 10-foot to 15-foot radius in 1951/52, with the same objectives in mind. The bigger crease allowed the goaltender more room to work and a better chance to see incoming shots; larger face-off circles spread out the players waiting for the puck to drop, increasing the opportunities for a player to

Ken Morrow of the Islanders attempts to clear Brian Hunter of the Oilers from Billy Smith's crease.

develop from the face-off. A further rule change in 1964/65 forbade any body contact during face-offs, forcing the players to the puck and not just tie one another up while the dropped puck sat on the ice.

The success of the Montreal Canadiens in scoring with a man advantage led to a modification of the penalty rules in 1956/57. Previous to this time, a team assessed a two-minute penalty played a man short until the two minutes had expired, even if the opposing team scored several times with the man advantage. The new rule stated that a penalized player would be allowed to return to the ice if the opposing team scored during his two minute penalty time. Even if he returned with time remaining in his penalty, his record would indicate two penalty minutes. In effect, the rule limited the damage that could be caused by a minor penalty to one goal against or a two-minute manpower disadvantage. Major penalties were unaffected by this rule; here, the offending team would play shorthanded for the entire five-minute duration of the penalty, regardless of any goals scored.

Substitutions were allowed on coincidental major penalties beginning in 1966/67. This new rule allowed teams to play with five skaters on the ice even if several players had received majors. Because coincidental majors were most commonly employed to punish players involved in fights, this rule change eliminated those situations where teams played three-on-three for five minutes after two players from each side got into a scuffle. It eliminated any possibilty of players on fast-skating teams fighting to obtain the strategic advantage of reducing the number of skaters on the ice. A similar rule governing coincidental minors was instituted in 1985.

The coming of age of television was reflected in hockey's rule changes. Standardized signals were adopted for referees in 1946 and linesmen in 1956, the ice surface was painted white to make the puck easier to follow in 1950 and a convention of wearing colored uniforms at home and white uniforms on the road was adopted in 1951. (In subsequent years this convention was reversed.)

ABOVE: *Henri Richard checks a Ranger during a game at Madison Square Garden.* BELOW: *Frank Mahovlich and Jean Beliveau tussle in the* penalty box as Ab McDonald joins in the melee. RIGHT: *Dallas Smith of the Bruins in a highsticking contest with the Islanders.*

A Home for the Hall

The Hockey Hall of Fame, founded in 1943, opened its first permanent home on the ground of the Canadian National Exhibition in Toronto in 1961. The modern-style building that housed the Hall was constructed as a result of cooperation between the NHL, whose member clubs funded construction, the city of Toronto, which provided the site, and the Canadian National Exhibition Association, which provided ongoing building maintenance.

Two of hockey's dynasty builders took a direct hand in construction. Conn Smythe, owner of the Toronto Maple Leafs, and Frank Selke, general manager of the Montreal Canadiens, arranged financing and supervised construction.

The United States Hockey Hall of Fame was chartered in 1968. Located in Eveleth, Minnesota, the Hall was established with the endorsement and cooperation of the Amateur Hockey Association of the United States.

The Hockey Hall of Fame in 1963, with curator Bobby Hewitson.

On the International Front

The game of ice hockey had firm roots in Europe, finding particular favor in Nordic and Alpine countries. It had been part of Olympic competition since 1924 (although there is controversy over the 1920 'Olympic' competition). In addition, an annual championship tournament staged by the sport's governing body, the International Ice Hockey Federation (IIHF), brought together the world's top hockey nations and determined a world amateur champion.

The World Championship and Olympics didn't allow professionals to compete, so the NHL, which employed the vast majority of the world's top players, didn't participate. The United States and the European nations sent national amateur teams to the championships. As most NHLers were Canadians, Canada sent the team that won the Allan Cup senior amateur championship trophy. In the 1940s and 1950s, senior hockey was an alternative to minor professional hockey that still provided some opportunity for players to advance to the NHL. With NHL jobs so scarce, good senior teams were a sort of advanced finishing school for gifted players after their junior hockey years and also were, in many cases, town or company-sponsored teams tied to their communities. In the 1950s, these clubs usually won the World Championship.

The Lethbridge Maple Leafs, Edmonton Mercurys, Penticton V's, Whitby Dunlops, Belleville McFarlands and Trail Smoke Eaters were all World Champions, but a new, emerging hockey power made town teams from small Canadian centers obsolete.

ABOVE: *Canada and Switzerland in a match at the St Moritz ice arena.*
BELOW: *The Canadian and Swedish national teams pose together at the St Moritz ice arena.*

RIGHT: *The 1953/54 Canadian team that lost to the Soviet Union.*
BELOW RIGHT: *The 1939 World Champion Trail Smoke Eaters were coached by Ab Crowie.*

PENTICTON V'S

CLIFF GREYELL EXECUTIVE · JACK McINTYRE · DINO MASCOTTO · GEORGE McAVOY CAPTAIN · KEV CONWAY · RON MONTGOMERY · ART SCHELL EXECUTIVE

BERNIE BATHGATE · JIM FAIRBURN · DON BERRY · ALLAN CUP · DOUG KILBURN · JACK McDONALD · ERNIE RUCKS

CANADIAN SENIOR AMATEUR HOCKEY CHAMPIONS

HARRY HARRIS TRAINER · IVAN McLELLAND · DICK WARWICK · GRANT WARWICK PLAYING COACH · BILL WARWICK · HAL GORDON · GEORGE CADY MANAGER

1953-1954

HAYES RICHARDS EXECUTIVE · DR. JACK STAPLETON EXECUTIVE · JIM THOM EXECUTIVE · CLEM BIRD PRESIDENT · MIKE MANGAN SECRETARY · HAROLD McINNES VICE-PRESIDENT · DR. BILL WHITE CLUB PHYSICIAN · C. LISO WINTERS EXECUTIVE

The Soviet Union had taken up the game of hockey in the late 1940s, building on their traditional sport of bandy, which was played on frozen soccer fields. Beginning in 1954, the Soviets entered their national team in the annual world championships, winning in their first attempt and finishing in the medals in seven of the next eight competitions. In 1963 the Soviets won again and owned the gold medal for the next nine years. The Soviets were a true national team that worked and trained together with full state support. They played a swirling, highly patterned game that required precision execution and tremendous physical conditioning to succeed. By the mid-1960s, it was obvious that the Soviet Nationals were one of the world's great hockey teams. Their showdown with NHLers wouldn't come until 1972, when this assumption was confirmed.

Canada tried to counter the power of the Soviet Nationals with its own national team based in Winnipeg. The national team program was headed by Father David Bauer and provided college scholarships to promising young players who were prepared to delay their opportunity to play in the NHL to play for Canada. These teams were good – far better than the senior clubs that had previously played for Canada – but the Soviets, Czechs and Swedes were improving at an even more rapid rate.

LEFT: *Jack McCartan in goal for the Rangers in 1961. McCartan played for the US team that won the gold medal at Squaw Valley in 1960.*

ABOVE: *Valeri Kharlamov of the Russian Army Team in action against the Rangers in 1975/76.*

The best results achieved by the Canadian Nationals were bronze medals in 1966, 1967 and 1968.

The United States National Team engineered a stunning upset of its own in 1960 when, at the Squaw Valley, California, Winter Olympics, the Americans won the gold medal. Canada and the Soviets were favored, but tremendous goaltending by Jack McCartan gave the Americans a 2-1 win over Canada and held his team in the game until it could rally to defeat the Soviets, 3-2. The American team also finished third in 1962.

The American college hockey system, which had grown into an important talent pool for both the NHL and the US National Team, put down its roots in the 1950s and 1960s. When big-league hockey expanded in the 1960s, 1970s and 1980s, college hockey slowly but steadily earned its credentials as a player development system equal to that of the traditional source of talent, Canadian junior hockey.

PART IV

The Modern Age

1967-Present

New Growth

On 6 June 1967, the most ambitious expansion program in sports history became a reality. The National Hockey League doubled in size, with six new teams each stocked with 20 players drafted from the Original Six clubs and their farm systems. The new clubs were established as the NHL's West Division, with the original teams forming the East. A 74-game schedule was adopted.

Some big-name players changed teams in the expansion draft. Goalie Glenn Hall joined the St Louis Blues while veteran Terry Sawchuk became the property of the Los Angeles Kings. Former Hart Trophy winner Andy Bathgate went from the New York Rangers to the Pittsburgh Penguins, while the Minnesota North Stars used their first draft pick to take Dave Balon from Montreal. Two former defensemen with the Toronto Maple Leafs, Bob Baun and Kent Douglas, took their rugged style of play to the California Seals, while the Philadelphia Flyers acquired two young goaltenders in Bernie Parent and Doug Favell.

LEFT: *Bernie Parent was a brilliant goalie with the Philadelphia Flyers. Opposing teams were often frustrated by their inability to get the puck past Parent. He led the Flyers to two Stanley Cup victories but his career was cut short due to a severe eye injury occurring in a game with the Rangers.*
RIGHT: *The Masterton Memorial Trophy is named after Minnesota forward Bill Masterton, who died of injuries sustained in a game in 1968.*

RIGHT: *Bruce MacGregor and Ted Irvin of the New York Rangers battle for the puck with the Pittsburgh Penguins during the early days of the expansion. Pittsburgh would later change their uniform colors to black and yellow to match the Pirates baseball team and the Steelers football team.*

The first match between an established club and one of the league's new arrivals saw the Montreal Canadiens defeat the Pittsburgh Penguins 2-1. Montreal superstar Jean Beliveau scored his four hundredth goal in this contest.

The expansion teams fared poorly against their established rivals, finishing the year with 40 wins, 86 losses and 18 ties. Red Kelly's Los Angeles Kings had the best record against the Original Six clubs, with 10 wins, 12 losses and two ties. The defending Stanley Cup Champion Toronto Maple Leafs fell out of playoff contention largely due to an unimpressive 10-11-3 record against the new West Division, while the New York Rangers finished second in the East, propelled by a fine 17-4-3 mark against the West as flashy linemates Jean Ratelle and Rod Gilbert enjoyed great success.

By mid-season, the California Seals were renamed the Oakland Seals in an attempt to foster greater community identification for an expansion franchise that was not doing well at the gate. Despite repeated rumors that the club was going to be shifted to Vancouver, the potential for national television revenue in the United States encouraged ownership to stick it out in Oakland.

Near the season's halfway mark, journeyman player Bill Masterton was fatally injured after striking his head on the ice. Masterton was a longtime minor pro player who was enjoying his first NHL season with the Minnesota North Stars when the accident occurred. The freakish nature of the incident – no rough play was involved – accelerated the trend that today sees almost universal use of helmets for skaters at the NHL level (helmets are now mandatory for new players; only players under the 'grandfather clause' are exempt).

Montreal finished first in the East, four points ahead of the Rangers. The Prince of Wales Trophy, formerly awarded to the team finishing first in regular-season play, was awarded to the team that won the East. The Original Six team enjoying the greatest improvement was Boston, which made the playoffs for the first time in the 1960s. The emergence of sophomore defenseman Bobby Orr and the acquisition by trade of Phil Esposito, Ken Hodge and Fred Stanfield from Chicago revital-

ized the Bruins and provided them with the nucleus of a contending team. The Philadelphia Flyers won the inaugural regular-season in the West Division, finishing one point up on Los Angeles. A new trophy, the Clarence Campbell Bowl, was awarded to the winner in the West. Minnesota North Stars' Wayne Connelly led all goal-scorers in the West Division with 35 markers.

Chicago's Stan Mikita won his fourth scoring title in five seasons, and repeated his feat of winning three NHL individual awards: the Art Ross Trophy as top scorer, the Lady Byng as most gentlemanly player and the Hart as most valuable player. The Montreal tandem of Gump Worsley and Rogatien Vachon won the Vezina Trophy as top netminders. Two Bruins were award-winners, as Bobby Orr won his first of eight consecutive Norris Trophies as top defenseman and Derek Sanderson was awarded the Calder Trophy as top rookie in the NHL.

The first all-star team had Worsley in goal with Orr and Tim Horton of Toronto on defense. Forwards were Mikita at center with Bobby Hull of Chicago and Detroit's Gordie Howe on the wings. Howe celebrated his fortieth birthday with no signs of slowing down, as he recorded 39 goals for the year.

The new Stanley Cup playoff format provided for interdivisional playoffs involving the first four teams in the East and West Divisions. Once two division champions were determined, a Stanley Cup final would be played between the two Division winners. St Louis, backstopped by veteran goaltender Glenn Hall, won in the West, while Montreal won the East. The Canadiens swept the Blues in four straight games to win the first Stanley Cup in an expanded NHL, but the Blues made every game close, taking two into overtime. Goaltender Hall won the Conn Smythe Trophy as the playoff MVP. St Louis would reach the finals and then be swept in four straight games in each of the first three post-expansion seasons.

The new double-size NHL was a reality. The new clubs had met with varying success at the ticket window and on the ice, but the long process of organization building and franchise stabilization was launched.

FAR RIGHT: *Bobby Orr had a profound effect on the style of play in the NHL, making defense more of an offensive position. Bobby Orr played from 1966 until 1979 when chronic knee problems forced his early retirement.*

RIGHT: *The Oakland Seals, an expansion club seen here playing the Red Wings, never did well and after a decade the franchise was moved to Cleveland and became the Cleveland Barons.*

Sabres, Canucks and the Big Bad Bruins

The NHL added two more teams in 1970/71. The Buffalo Sabres, playing in the old Memorial Auditorium, joined the league, as did the Vancouver Canucks. Despite Vancouver's location on Canada's Pacific coast, both teams were placed in the East Division. Chicago, winners of the East Division regular season the year before, was shifted to the West. The Boston Bruins were riding high after winning the Cup in 1969/70 and were highly favored to repeat in 1970/71. The club had acquired a reputation as the 'Big Bad Bruins' for their rambunctious, hard-nosed play. They were a scoring machine unlike any seen in the NHL to that time, with center Phil Esposito dominating the area in front of the opposing goaltender and rearguard Bobby Orr laying in hard, low accurate shots from the blueline. With an able supporting cast including John Bucyk, Wayne Cashman, Ken Hodge, Don Awrey, Ted Green and goaltender Gerry Cheevers, the Bruins scored 399 goals

LEFT: *Johnny Bucyk captained the Boston Bruins of the early 1970s when along with such other players as Wayne Cashman, Ken Hodge, Bobby Orr, Phil Esposito, Don Awrey and Gerry Cheevers, the team was an NHL powerhouse.*

RIGHT: *Bobby Orr, seen here tying up Philadelphia Flyer Rick McLeish.*

while winning 57 and tying seven for 121 points in 78 regular-season games. By comparison, Chicago, winners in the West, had the next most potent offense with 277 goals.

Esposito upped the single-season scoring record by 26 points, finishing with 76 goals and 76 assists for 152 points. Orr was next with 37 goals and an unheard of total of 102 assists for 139 points. Bruins Bucyk and Hodge were third and fourth in scoring. In fact seven of the top 11 scorers were Boston players. No club has ever dominated the scoring leader table like the 1970/71 Bruins.

ABOVE: *Ken Hodge was fourth overall in point scoring during the 1970/71 season.*

RIGHT: *Wayne Cashman, seen here late in his career, became team captain.*

The Upset of 1971

Boston, then, was heavily favored to repeat as Stanley Cup champions. The Montreal Canadiens upset the Bruins in a remarkable seven-game series that saw the emergence of Ken Dryden as a top-ranked goaltender. Dryden had been called up to the Canadiens from their AHL farm team in March and, after playing strongly in the club's previous six regular-season matches, got the call to tend goal in the playoffs. He played so well in the post-season that in addition to being part of a Stanley Cup winner, he won the Conn Smythe Trophy as playoff MVP.

Because of his limited regular-season play, Dryden qualified for and won the Calder Trophy as top rookie the following season, 1971/72.

Montreal's route to the Cup remained an arduous one once the Bruins were eliminated. The playoff format had been

BELOW: *A jubilant Ken Dryden drinks from the Stanley Cup.*

RIGHT: *Ken Dryden in goal for the Montreal Canadiens.*

Jean Ratelle, seen here with the New York Rangers in action against the Buffalo Sabres. Ratelle is a two-time winner of the Lady Byng Trophy for sportsmanship, winner of the Masterton Memorial Trophy, an NHL all-star and member of the Hockey Hall of Fame. Jean Ratelle and Brad Park would be traded to Boston in a move that would bring Phil Esposito and Carol Vadnais to the New York Rangers.

amended so that East and West Division clubs faced each other in the semifinals. Montreal needed six games to get by Minnesota. Chicago, now in the West, defeated the New York Rangers in seven games in the semifinals. The Montreal-Chicago Cup final also went seven games, with the Canadiens prevailing. Montreal captain Jean Beliveau retired after this series with 10 Stanley Cup victories.

The Bruins reacquired the Stanley Cup in 1971/72, finishing on top in the regular season and dominating the playoffs. Chicago continued to dominate in the West. Esposito and Orr again led the scoring parade, but the next three spots were occupied by Jean Ratelle, Vic Hadfield and Rod Gilbert, who were known as the G-A-G or Goal-A-Game line for the New York Rangers.

FAR LEFT: *Vic Hadfield was offered a million dollar contract to play for the WHA, but stayed with the Rangers.*
LEFT: *Canadien captain Jean Beliveau retired in 1970/71, having won the Stanley Cup on 10 occasions.*

BELOW: *Rod Gilbert played with Jean Ratelle and Vic Hadfield on the Goal-A-Game line for the Rangers.*

Hockey Night in Moscow

Lovers of hockey were treated to a rare circumstance in sport in September of 1972 — the first opportunity to see a team of NHL stars, Team Canada, play a playoff-style series against the national hockey team of the Soviet Union. What made this confrontation unique was that while both sides could lay claim to being the best hockey players in the world, they had never faced one another on the ice.

The Soviet Union had dominated hockey's world championship competitions and Winter Olympic tournaments since 1963, defeating other European national teams and the best amateur squads from Canada and the United States. Canadian hockey organizers, frustrated at the IIHF's refusal to allow even limited use of professional players in international play, and at the fact that the USSR's 'amateur' team was comprised of army officers, withdrew from further competition in 1969.

ABOVE: *In 1972 Team Canada played the Soviet Union in a playoff-style series and managed to beat the Russian team four games to three.*

RIGHT: *Team Canada on the blue line for the playing of the national anthems.*

Because Russia versus Canada had always been the great drawing card of international hockey, negotiations took place to stage a series on terms acceptable to both sides. The eventual format — eight games, four in Canada and four in the Soviet Union — saw the Soviets' best players face off against Team Canada, a squad made up of the best Canadian-born NHL players and coached by Harry Sinden of the Boston Bruins. Conspicuously excluded from the Team Canada roster was Bobby Hull, who had jumped to the fledgling World Hockey

The Soviet team rushes the puck up the ice past a Team Canada defender as the Russian audience looks on during a game in Moscow.

RIGHT: *Players from Team Canada celebrate scoring a goal against Russian goaltender Vladislav Tretiak.*

Association. Bobby Orr, an automatic selection to the roster, was lost to Team Canada because of recurring knee problems.

The sentiment in much of Canada was that the Soviets would be overwhelmed by Team Canada, but the reality of the confrontation was far different. Team Canada scored twice early in the first game, and it seemed that the pundits who forecast an easy time for the NHLers would be proven right, but the Soviets roared back to win by a score of 7-3. The Soviets showed a swirling attack, late-game conditioning and puck skills unlike anything seen in NHL play. Even when the Canadian defenders weren't fooled by the Soviet's maneuvers, the speed at which these moves were executed was simply too fast for the conventional NHL-style response. The Soviets left Canada leading in games two to one with one game tied. After the fourth and final game in Canada, when the media and the Canadian hockey establishment were trying to pin the blame for Team Canada's poor showing on the specific group of players gathered in 1972, Phil Esposito blasted the public's wavering support in a post-game television interview. With the benefit of hindsight, Esposito's speech indicated the realization on the part of the Team Canada players that they had to go out and beat a marvellous Soviet team on their own; 50 years of NHL excellence and tradition wouldn't put the puck in the net in Moscow. As well, Esposito's comments established him as a leader and, for the first time in his career, moved him out of the shadow that was a natural consequence of playing on a team dominated by the magnificent talents of Bobby Orr.

The European half of the series began with the Soviets winning the first Moscow contest 5-4. Team Canada, now in a very deep hole, responded with one of sport's finest team performances, clawing their way to three one-goal victories. They needed three third-period goals in the final game to win, and got them from Esposito, Yvan Cournoyer and, in the final minute of play, Paul Henderson. Canadian hockey fans have burned into their memories the image of Henderson embraced by Cournoyer as the puck rested in the Soviet net behind goaltender Vladislav Tretiak.

Team Canada won the series four games to three, with one game tied. Paul Henderson of the Toronto Maple Leafs had the game-winning goal in each of the last three games.

Despite the narrow win, North American professional hockey could not help but learn from the skills of the Soviets and other top European teams. Swedes, Finns and Czechs gradually found their way onto the rosters of most NHL clubs, and European-style coaching strategies and training methods are now a part of everyday life in modern professional hockey.

Further exhibitions and tournament competition between NHLers and European national or club teams have resulted in some inspiring games. The Montreal Canadiens and the Soviet Red Army played to a 3-3 tie on New Year's Eve 1975 in a game many experts consider one of the most exciting ever played. Team Canada played well to beat both the Soviet and Czech nationals in the first six-nation Canada Cup tournament in September of 1976. The Soviets demonstrated their capacity to modify their game almost in mid-stride when, trailing 4-2 in the second game of the 1979 Challenge Cup between the NHL all-stars and the Soviet nationals, they scored three quick goals and then held the NHL's best to a total of six shots on goal in the third period. And, in the Canada Cup of 1984, Team Canada defeated the Soviets on Mike Bossy's overtime goal set up by John Tonelli and Paul Coffey.

BELOW: *Phil Esposito rushes the puck past a Soviet player as the Russian bench looks on.*

RIGHT: *Mikhajlov of the Soviet national team holds the 1979 Challenge Cup aloft.*

The College Victory

But these thrilling games can do no more than equal the miracle victory by the US Olympic team over the Soviets during the 1980 Winter Olympics in Lake Placid, New York. The Soviets were reigning world champions and had beaten the American team 11-3 in an exhibition game just a few days before the Games. The American team, made up of college players and coached by Herb Brooks from the University of Minnesota, played an inspired game and wholly deserved their 4-3 win over the Soviets. This victory raised the profile of

Mark Johnson of the US Olympic team forechecks the puck away from Maltsev of the Soviet team during the 1980 winter Olympic games at Lake Placid, New York.

ABOVE LEFT: *Players from the US and Soviet teams become entangled as they watch the puck bounce free.*
LEFT: *Herb Brooks coached the US team to a gold medal in the 1980 Olympics, and would go on to coach the New York Rangers.*

ABOVE: *Jim Craig played goal for the US team in 1980, and went on to play pro for the Atlanta Flames.*

the sport of hockey in the United States. It served as the final legitimization of US college hockey as a development pool for the NHL and catapulted a number of players from the victorious US team (Jim Craig, Neal Broten, Dave Silk, Rob McClanahan, Ken Morrow and others) directly into the NHL.

Today professional hockey is played in Scandinavia and the Alpine countries of Europe while the Soviets and Czechs continue their excellent full-time 'amateur' programs. American colleges, and European junior and senior clubs and national teams have joined Canadian major junior hockey as the main talent providers for the NHL.

Of the 504 players drafted by NHL clubs in 1985 and 1986, 130 were US college or high school players and 58 were Europeans.

The US Olympic hockey team members congratulate one another on a victory during the 1980 winter Olympic games.

Expansion and the WHA

Two more clubs joined the NHL in 1972/73: the Atlanta Flames in the West Division and the New York Islanders in the East. Montreal won the East and the Stanley Cup while Chicago again finished first in the West. Philadelphia and Minnesota greatly reduced the Black Hawks' margin in the West Division standings, an indication of approaching parity between the Original Six clubs and the 'Second Six' added in 1967/68. The Esposito-Orr lock on the top two spots in the scoring race was broken by an expansion player – Bobby Clarke of the Flyers, who finished second. Clarke's Philadelphia teammate, Rick MacLeish, finished fourth.

A second major professional hockey league – the World Hockey Association – commenced operations with the 1972/73 season. The WHA extended to the sport of hockey the notion of rival professional leagues that had already been pioneered by the American Football League and the American Basketball Association. In fact two of the WHA's enterprising founders, Gary Davidson and Dennis Murphy, had been involved in the ABA start-up as well. The WHA operated over seven seasons, from 1972 to 1979. During that time it fielded 32 different teams in 24 cities, of which all but four faded away. The survivors – the Edmonton Oilers, Hartford Whalers, Quebec Nordiques and Winnipeg Jets – went on to become part of the NHL.

LEFT: *Bobby Clarke, the captain of the Philadelphia Flyers, won the Frank J Selke Trophy, Hart Memorial Trophy, Lester Patrick Trophy, Masterton Trophy, was an NHL all-star and two-time winner of the Stanley Cup.*
BELOW: *The Quebec Nordiques of the WHA.*

The quality of WHA hockey rang in a half-notch below that of the NHL in the new league's first few seasons, but by the late seventies, WHA teams would have been competitive in the NHL. The establishment of the new league served almost every professional hockey player, whether he was on a WHA payroll or not. The sudden emergence of a rival employer caused player salaries to rise dramatically as everyone from stars to minor leaguers to talented junior players were courted by the new league. Careers were extended throughout hockey. Many stars jumped from the NHL to the new league. Crossing over were Bobby Hull, Gordie Howe, JC Tremblay, Marc Tardif, Bernie Parent, Derek Sanderson, Dave Keon, Frank Mahovlich and others.

The WHA hastened the introduction of European players and the European style to North America. The Winnipeg Jets, in addition to signing the WHA's ticket to instant credibility, Bobby Hull, iced as many as nine Swedish or Finnish players

in 1976/77 and played a crowd-pleasing, swirling European-inspired style that won the WHA's championship Avco Cup on three occasions. The 'Luxury Line' of Hull with Ulf Nilsson and Anders Hedberg was one of the world's best in the mid-seventies. The WHA also played frequent exhibition matches with eastern European teams. Winnipeg traveled to Moscow to play in a tournament and in 1977/78, a Czech and a Russian team played one game each against all WHA clubs that counted in the regular-season standings.

As big as Bobby Hull's defection to the WHA was the signing of 46-year-old Gordie Howe and his two sons, Mark and Marty, by the Houston Aeros in 1973. Gordie Howe, retired for two years after 25 glorious seasons with the Detroit Red Wings, enjoyed considerable success with Houston and later, New England, in the WHA. Howe's all-star selections and his 100-point seasons in the WHA were used by the league's critics as an indication of the poor quality of WHA play. But observers of

LEFT: *Goalie Bernie Parent played for the WHA before settling down with the Flyers.*

RIGHT: *The New York Golden Blades of the WHA folded when the league went bust. Only the Edmonton Oilers, Winnipeg Jets, Quebec Nordiques and New England Whalers survived.*

ABOVE: *Bobby Hull jumped to the WHA and played for the Winnipeg Jets and the Hartford Whalers. When the Whalers became an NHL team, Hull played along with Gordie Howe, where they both finished their playing careers.*

RIGHT: *Bobby Hull of Winnipeg and Gordie Howe of the Houston Aeros gave the WHA great credibility when they both jumped from the NHL. Unfortunately for the WHA, even the influx of such playing greats couldn't keep the league alive.*

Howe in the WHA and throughout his five-decade NHL career recognized the touch of the master craftsman and tactician. In the very last years of his career, Gordie described his play as 'poetry in slow motion,' but even in his last season when the Whalers joined the NHL, Howe played in all 80 games and scored 15 goals despite being hampered by a bad wrist and going on 52 years of age.

Wayne Gretzky joined the WHA's Indianapolis Racers at the start of what was to prove to be the league's final season. As a 17-year-old rookie, Gretzky recorded 110 points in the WHA, transferring from Indianapolis to Edmonton early in the season. Again those who decried the level of talent in the WHA pointed to Gretzky's success as an indication of how poor the WHA was. After all, it was obvious that Wayne Gretzky was too frail to succeed in *real* big-league hockey.

The on-again off-again merger talks between NHL and WHA representatives finally clicked after the 1978/79 season, allowing Edmonton, Hartford, Quebec and Winnipeg to join the senior league. The price of entry for the new teams was steep, but, finally, big-league hockey in North America was a one-league proposition again.

RIGHT: *Gordie Howe, seen here with the Hartford Whalers, played professionally through three decades.*

BELOW: *The New England Whalers of the WHA would enter the NHL as the Hartford Whalers.*

The Bullies of Broad Street

ABOVE: *Fred Shero coached the Philadelphia Flyers to two Stanley Cup victories before moving on to coach the Rangers.*

RIGHT: *Reggie Leach scored 19 playoff goals in 1976.*

The old order of the NHL was rocked by more than just defections to the WHA. In 1973/74 the Philadelphia Flyers became the first expansion club to win the Stanley Cup. The Flyers engineered their victory by taking the tactics of the Big Bad Bruins of the early seventies one better — they were the masters of intimidation, clutch, grab and grapple hockey. In a sense they were the ultimate professional hockey club. They did whatever it took to win. This philosophy resulted in a hockey club that took a lot of penalties and killed them effectively. Coach Fred Shero mixed training methods designed to counteract the boredom of the season's long grind with a bunch of what he called his 'knuckle boys' and several talented role players. To this combination he had the good fortune to be able to add goaltender Bernie Parent, who was on the verge of playing the best hockey of his life, center and team captain Bobby Clarke, the most determined player in the NHL, and ultra-sharpshooter Reggie Leach. The result wasn't what hockey purists called art, but it got Shero and the Flyers' names engraved on the Stanley Cup.

Fans around the NHL loved the mayhem wrought by the Flyers. They were the biggest draw in the league throughout the 1970s, and even though 'rock 'em sock 'em' hockey hasn't been the way to the Cup since the mid-seventies Flyers were

163

known as the 'Broad Street Bullies,' their influence is still felt. Bobby Clarke, now known as Bob, became the Flyers' general manager in 1985, and though the club is now constructed along different lines, they still play with a lot of heart in a style that delights their own, particular kind of fans. Hockey games in Philadelphia's Spectrum are unlike those in any other NHL arena. The lights, the scoreboard and the programs all combine to involve the fans and make them feel that the Flyers are something special and theirs alone.

The Flyers won the West in 1973/74, finishing with 112 points. Boston had 113 in the East. Bruins Esposito, Hodge, Orr and Cashman led all scorers, with Bobby Clarke fifth. In winning the Cup, Philadelphia swept Atlanta in four straight games, won a seven-game semifinal against the New York Rangers and then repeated this feat by winning four of seven from the Big Bad Bruins in the finals. Game seven ended 1-0 for Philadelphia, as an enraged Bobby Orr watched most of the last two minutes of the game from the penalty box as his club was thwarted from getting a tying goal. Throughout the long season and playoffs, goaltender Bernie Parent was the very embodiment of consistency. The stingy Flyer defensive style — it was physically dangerous to try and set up in front of the Philadelphia goal — enabled Parent to record a goals-against average of 1.89 in the regular season and 2.02 in the playoffs. The Flyers had yanked hockey into a new era.

LEFT: *Center Bobby Clarke follows the game as he waits to exit the penalty box.*
BELOW: *Phil Esposito, seen here with Boston, also played for Chicago and the New York Rangers.*

RIGHT: *Wayne Cashman was the fourth leading scorer in the NHL in 1973/74.*

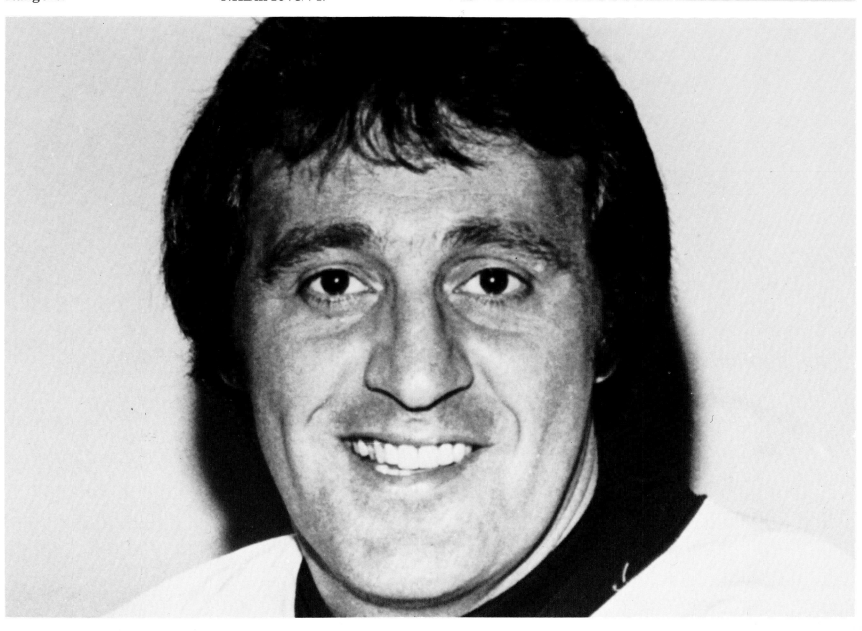

Conference Time

The NHL became an 18-team circuit in 1974/75. Added to the league were the Kansas City Scouts and the Washington Capitals. The East/West divisional alignment in place since 1967 was scrapped, and was replaced with a structure that featured two conferences made up of two divisions each. These divisions were named after some of the great builders of the NHL. The Prince of Wales Conference was comprised of the Charles F Adams and James Norris Divisions. The Clarence Campbell Conference was made up of the Lester Patrick and the Conn Smythe Divisions.

The trophies formerly awarded to regular-season standings winners from the old East and West Divisions were now awarded to the Conference champions as determined by play-off performances. Twelve teams now qualified for post-season play. The first-place teams in each division advanced to the quarterfinals, while the second- and third-place teams in each division played a short, three-game preliminary series that determined the playoff opponents for the four division winners. The quarterfinals determined the division champions; the semifinals the conference victors. The two conference champions would then meet in the Stanley Cup final.

The regular season now consisted of 80 games and hockey fans had four divisional races to watch. Three divisions were won by teams finishing with 113 points – Philadelphia in the Patrick, Buffalo in the Adams and Montreal in the Norris. The Sabres were powered by the French Connection line of Gil Perreault, Rene Robert and Rick Martin. This high-scoring trio netted 131 goals and 196 points, as Buffalo upped its scoring output by more than 100 goals in the regular season. Never having finished higher than fourth, Buffalo jumped 25

BELOW LEFT: *Guy Charron with the Washington Capitals in 1975.*
BELOW: *The Kansas City Scouts did poorly and moved on to become the Colorado Rockies.*

RIGHT: *Rick Martin played with Rene Robert and Gil Perreault on the 'French Connection Line.'*

points in the standings over its previous best season. The Sabres liked their defensemen large; Bill Hajt, Jocelyn Guevremont, Jim Schoenfeld and Gerry Korab all eclipsed six feet and 200 pounds.

An even greater improvement in regular season standings was enjoyed by the New York Islanders, who climbed from a sorry 30 points in their first season to 88 points in their third. This represented a dizzying ascent to respectability, which was enhanced by the Islanders' strong showing in the playoffs, where they extended the defending-champion Flyers to seven games.

The Los Angeles Kings also made great strides, finishing second to Montreal in the Norris Division with 105 points. The Kings achieved this consistent performance with a balanced attack and strong goaltending from Rogie Vachon and Gary Edwards. In June of 1975, the Kings acquired Marcel Dionne in a trade with Detroit. Dionne would go on to become Los Angeles' most durable and successful performer. In 1986 he passed Phil Esposito to become the NHL's second leading scorer, trailing only Gordie Howe. Montreal fans rejoiced on the coming of age of Guy Lafleur. This junior superstar was the Canadiens' much-heralded first draft pick in 1971 and in his

LEFT: *Gil Perreault stickhandles past a New York Islander en route to a goal.*
ABOVE: *Marcel Dionne played for Detroit and Los Angeles before being traded to the Rangers in 1987.*

RIGHT: *Jim Schoenfeld played defense for the Buffalo Sabres and eventually became team captain.*

first three seasons with the Canadiens, played decent, inconspicuous hockey. Finally, in the 1974/75 campaign, the patience of the Canadiens' management was rewarded as Lafleur emerged as a genuine superstar; a game-breaking 50-goal scorer that made everybody on the ice with him a better hockey player. Strangely, this blossoming coincided with Lafleur's decision to stop wearing a helmet and let his moderately long blond hair stream behind him as he raced down his wing.

In the 1975 Prince of Wales Conference semifinals Buffalo eliminated Montreal in six games. The Stanley Cup finals came down to the Flyers and the Sabres, with Philadelphia prevailing. This series came to be known as the Fog Bowl, as hot spring weather in Buffalo resulted in games three and four being frequently delayed to disperse a dense mist that rose from the ice surface. The Flyers' recipe for success on the glass remained the same: hard, intimidating, desire-laden hockey and stellar goaltending from Bernie Parent. It appeared that an aggressive, penalty-filled style was the route to championship hockey in the National Hockey League of the 1970s.

Flowering in Montreal

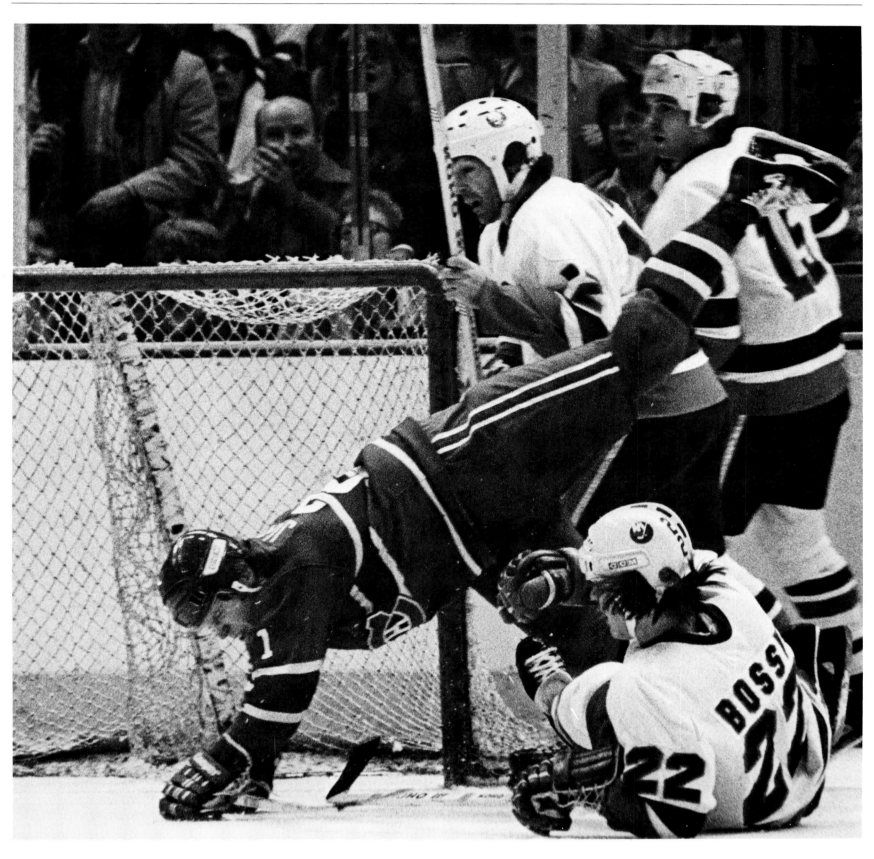

LEFT: *Guy Lafleur would become a Montreal superstar in the 1970s.*

ABOVE: *Doug Jarvis of the Canadiens and Mike Bossy of the Islanders go flying as JP Parise and Billy Harris chase the puck.*

With two Stanley Cups under their belts, the Flyers seemed poised to establish a hockey dynasty, but Montreal, with Lafleur now on track, entered the 1975/76 season with the objective of reclaiming the Cup. The Canadiens were a talent-laden team strong in all facets of the game. Lafleur combined with Steve Shutt and Pete Mahovlich on the top scoring line, with Jacques Lemaire and Yvon Cournoyer providing additional experience and savvy. In Jimmy Roberts, Bob Gainey and Doug Jarvis, the Habs had a peerless checking line capable of shutting down the opposition's top scorers. On defense, the

LEFT: *Serge Savard and Larry Robinson discuss strategy before a face-off.*

BELOW: *Steve Shutt played with Guy Lafleur and Pete Mahovlich on a very high scoring line for the Canadiens in the 1970s.*

Canadiens were blessed with three of the best in the game in Serge Savard, Guy Lapointe and Larry Robinson. All three were big men with heavy shots and playmaking skills. In goal, Ken Dryden, the hero in the Canadiens' upset Cup win in 1971, was ready to stop whatever breached Montreal's strong defense.

The Canadiens finished with 127 points; the Flyers 118. The showdown came in the Stanley Cup finals, where the Habs won going away, sweeping Philadelphia in four straight games. Even Kate Smith's live performance of 'God Bless America' (the Flyer's good luck charm) failed to stop the Canadiens. Montreal won 12 of 13 playoff games that year, with their severest test coming from the young New York Islanders and their rookie-of-the-year, Bryan Trottier.

ABOVE: *Yvon Cournoyer had exceptional skating speed and became a scoring threat for the Canadiens of the 1970s.*

RIGHT: *Guy Lapointe was just one of a number of great defencemen that made up the Canadiens of the 1970s.*

'The Trade'

Midway through the 1975/76 season the NHL was rocked with what came to be known around the league as 'The Trade.' On 7 November 1975, Boston traded Phil Esposito and defenseman Carol Vadnais to the New York Rangers for Brad Park and Jean Ratelle. Park was a fixture on defense for the Rangers and a five-time all-star when he was swapped to the Bruins. Ratelle was the classy centerman on the Goal-A-Game line and epitomized the Rangers' style. It was by far the biggest NHL deal since Toronto traded Frank Mahovlich, Pete Stemkowski and Carl Brewer to Detroit for Norm Ullman, Paul Henderson and Floyd Smith in 1968.

Both clubs benefitted from the exchange. The Rangers acquired some toughness in the slot from Esposito and a solid performer in Vadnais. The Bruins obtained six excellent seasons from Ratelle and a leader on defense in Brad Park, who even managed to make the NHL all-star team in the season in which he was traded.

In a move equally significant to hockey's business side, John A Ziegler, Jr succeeded Clarence Campbell as president of the National Hockey League.

LEFT: *Brad Park, seen here as a Ranger, would play for Boston and Detroit before retiring.*

RIGHT: *Jean Ratelle was elected to the Hall of Fame in 1985.*

Bobby Orr

Park's acquisition by the Bruins acknowledged the unfortunate state of Bobby Orr's fragile knees. Orr remade the defenseman's position, factoring it into his club's offense like never before. He was the first NHL defenseman to win the league's scoring championship in 1969/70 and, with Phil Esposito, took the Bruins from also-rans to champions. He was an all-star team selection in nine consecutive seasons and won the James Norris Trophy as the NHL's top defenseman eight straight times. In all he had six operations performed on his knees. After the 1974/75 season, he played in only 36 games over the next four campaigns. His last great showing was in the 1976 Canada Cup international tournament where, despite limited mobility, he was instrumental in Canada's victory. He finished his hockey career as a member of the Chicago Black Hawks, playing six games in 1978/79. He retired in November of 1978. At its next meeting, the selection committee of the Hockey Hall of Fame waived its customary five-year waiting period and inducted Orr into the Hall in September of 1979.

BELOW: *Bobby Orr in the familiar black and yellow Number 4 for Boston.*

RIGHT: *Bobby Orr, seen here at the end of his career playing for the Chicago Black Hawks.*

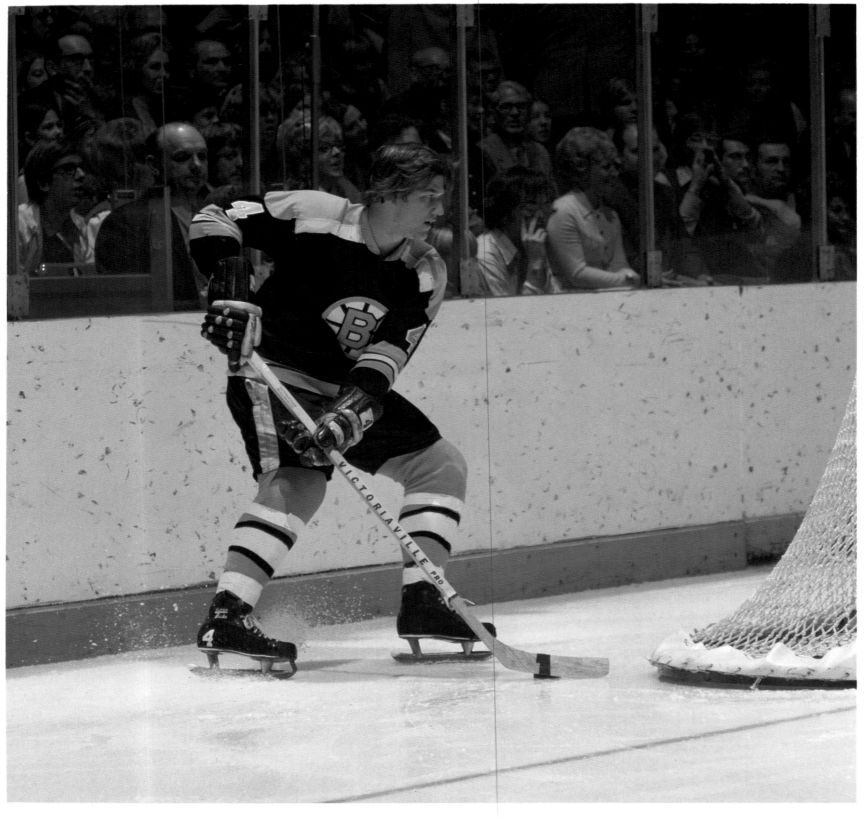

Montreal's Seventies Dynasty

Beginning with their Cup win in 1976, the Canadiens dealt pure intimidation-style hockey a crippling blow. The Habs went on to reel off four consecutive Cup wins, establishing a modern dynasty exceeded only by earlier editions of les Canadiens, which won the Cup from 1956 to 1960. Through this run, Lafleur was the NHL's virtuoso performer, posting six consecutive 50-goal performances and all-star team selections. He became no less than what the fans demanded of him: the worthy successor to Beliveau and Richard. The Canadiens, coached by Scotty Bowman, were rarely out-played and even more rarely defeated. During their four-year reign as Cup champions, the Habs lost only 55 of 320 regular-season games. They lost only eight games in the 1976/77 season, finishing with a league-record 132 points. Some hockey experts felt

Bowman had only to open the gate and let his ultra-talented athletes take the ice, but he recognized his job as one of keeping his players on edge and anxious to succeed. He juggled his lines and varied his players' responsibilities with great success. The players stayed hungry.

On 11 May 1979 the Canadiens received the stiffest challenge in their four years of supremacy in the NHL. The Boston Bruins took them to a seventh and deciding game in the semi-

LEFT: *Yvon Lambert helped create the winning goal of the 1979 Stanley Cup semifinal against Boston in overtime.*

BELOW: *Guy Lafleur stickhandles past Bryan Trottier of the Islanders as Larry Robinson looks on.*

ABOVE: *Rejean Houle played on the 1979 Stanley Cup champion Montreal Canadiens.*

RIGHT: *The 1979 Canadiens defeated the Rangers in the final series, four games to one, to win the Stanley Cup.*

finals and led 3-1 with 15 minutes of regulation time to play. Lafleur, playing at top pace, set up two clean goals by Mark Napier and Guy Lapointe. With less then four minutes remaining in the period, the Bruins took the lead on a goal by Rick Middleton. Lafleur again responded with a blazing 35-foot shot into the only puck-sized portion of the Boston net not covered by goaltender Gilles Gilbert. In overtime, after nine minutes of wide open action, it was the Canadiens' journeymen players, Rejean Houle, Mario Tremblay and Yvon Lambert, who created the winning goal. Montreal went on to defeat the New York Rangers four games to one in the Stanley Cup finals. The Canadians' dynasty of the 1970s stood one championship short of their remarkable record of exactly 20 years before.

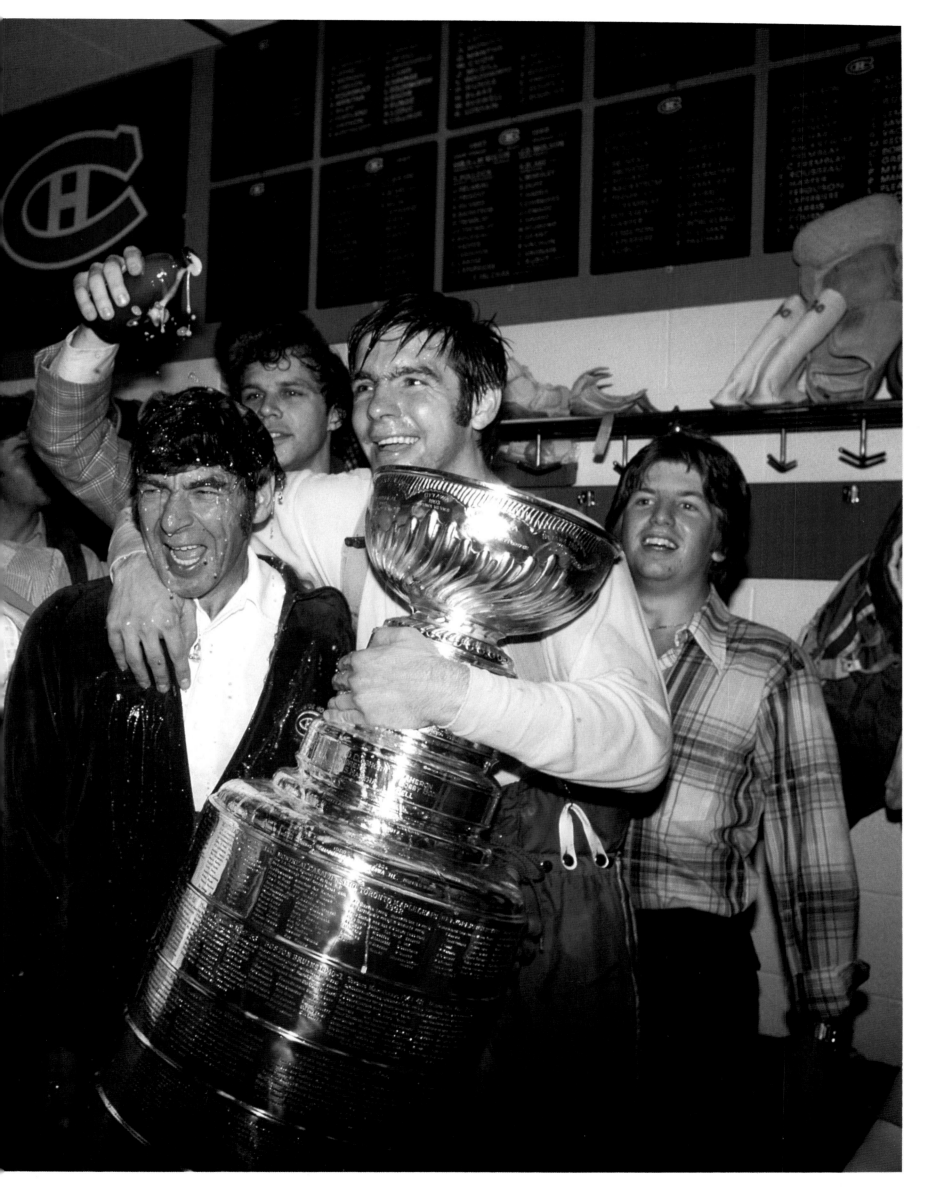

The Shifting Hands

Franchise maneuvering continued throughout the second half of the 1970s. In 1976/77, the California Seals franchise moved to Cleveland where it operated as the Cleveland Barons. In that same year, the Kansas City Scouts relocated to Denver where they were known as the Colorado Rockies. In 1978/79, the NHL sought to solve two problems by merging two wavering franchises: Cleveland and Minnesota. The North Stars acquired the contracts of all Barons' players, and leapt from 45 to 68 to 88 points in just two seasons. The following year, 1979/80, the WHA-NHL merger took place, with Edmonton, New England (now called Hartford), Quebec and Winnipeg making the NHL a 21-team circuit. Sixteen teams now qualified for the playoffs, as first-round byes for division winners were eliminated. Instead, at the end of the regular season the league's 21 clubs were ranked in order of points. The team finishing first played the team finishing sixteenth; the second-place team played the fifteenth and so on.

RIGHT: *Barry Beck played for the Colorado Rockies before moving on to play with the Rangers.*

BELOW: *The Cleveland Barons merged with the Minnesota North Stars, and the Barons went out of existence in 1978/79.*

Leave 'em to the Isles

ABOVE: *Bobby Nystrom would score the winning goal in the Islanders' first Stanley Cup victory in 1979/80.*

RIGHT: *Al Arbour coached the Islanders for 13 years, winning four consecutive Stanley Cups. He retired at the end of the 1985/86 season.*

Montreal would prove unable to win its fifth consecutive Stanley Cup in 1979/80. Instead, the New York Islanders, a team in only its eighth NHL season, defeated Philadelphia four games to two in the finals with Bob Nystrom scoring the Cup-winning goal for the Islanders in overtime.

By 1979 the Islanders had established themselves as an elite NHL team. The combination of Bill Torrey as general manager and Al Arbour, a former NHL defenceman, as head coach hoisted the Islanders over the 100-point barrier for four consecutive seasons beginning in 1975/76. The Islanders played so well in their five-game semifinal loss to the Canadiens that season, that it appeared to be only a matter of time before the Islanders would reach the Stanley Cup finals.

ABOVE: *Denis Potvin skates a victory lap with the Stanley Cup above his head.*
LEFT: *Mike Bossy holds the Islander record for most goals scored by a rookie, with 53.*

RIGHT: *Glenn 'Chico' Resch played well for the Islanders but was traded to Colorado. He played with the Devils before moving on to play goal for the Flyers.*

The team was a textbook example of how to build a hockey powerhouse through wise draft selections. Lorne Henning, Bob Nystrom, Denis Potvin, Clark Gillies, Bryan Trottier, Mike Bossy and John Tonelli were all selected in the entry draft by Bill Torrey from 1972 to 1977. These players, along with goaltenders Billy Smith and Glenn 'Chico' Resch, were the engine that drove the Islanders not just to the Stanley Cup championship in 1980, but in 1981, 1982 and 1983 as well. Like the Canadiens before them, the Islanders owned the Cup for four consecutive seasons.

It is Mike Bossy, perhaps more than any other player, who best exemplifies the Islander aesthetic. Though 14 other players were selected ahead of him in the 1977 entry draft, Bossy immediately found his range in the NHL. Right from his rookie year, he was a 50-goal shooter, surpassing this milestone in each of his first nine NHL seasons. In addition to four Stanley Cups and eight all-star selections, he won the Lady Byng Trophy for gentlemanly conduct three times. He is one of those skaters who isn't flashy. He's just fast. His shot is accurate and released with a lightning quickness. He is the ultimate hockey sniper, scoring at a pace beyond that of any other player to come before him in hockey. Only Wayne Gretzky accumulated goals at a rate that exceeded Bossy's.

From Mountain to Meadow

Franchise maneuvering didn't stop during the Islanders' reign. In 1980/81 the Atlanta club relocated to Calgary, retaining the Flames name. This shift of location put seven of the NHL's 21 clubs in Canadian cities. The following season, 1981/82, the league dropped its balanced schedule and realigned the divisional structure. This had two effects: the teams in each division were located close to one another and the number of games each team played against its divisional rivals was increased. This reduced travel costs and increased interest in divisional play. The playoffs now stayed within each team's division until a division champion was declared. Division champions played off for their Conference title, with the two conference champs meeting in the Stanley Cup finals. This has resulted in some great rivalries: Quebec-Montreal, Boston-Hartford, Philadelphia-Washington, Rangers-Islanders, Chicago-St Louis and Calgary-Edmonton.

In 1982/83 the Colorado Rockies were relocated to the Meadowlands in New Jersey, where they became known as the New Jersey Devils. The resulting shift of Winnipeg from the Norris to the Smythe Division and the addition of New Jersey to the Patrick Division, created an NHL consisting of three divisions of five clubs and one, the Patrick, of six.

LEFT: *Dan Bouchard in goal for the Atlanta Flames. Poor attendance forced the franchise to move to Calgary in 1980/81.*

BELOW: *The Colorado Rockies moved to New Jersey and were renamed the Devils. They are seen here playing the Islanders at the Brendan Byrne Arena in the Meadowlands.*

The Oilers' Boom

It is in Edmonton, a medium-sized city in northern Alberta, where the *NHL Official Guide and Record Book* came in for a rewrite. The Edmonton Oilers, one of the four surviving WHA franchises to merge with the NHL in 1979/80, built a team around the dazzling skills of Wayne Gretzky, the young center who has made a mockery of hockey's benchmarks of excellence. Since the addition of the 'Second Six' teams to the NHL in 1967/68, the trend in the NHL has been toward greater offense, as the number of goals scored per game has increased from approximately six to eight. But still, certain hallmarks of individual excellence remain: 50-goal and 100-point seasons being foremost. From 1917 to 1993, there have been 143

LEFT: *Wayne Gretzky is regarded as the greatest hockey player of all time, breaking records season after season.*

BELOW: *Wayne Gretzky stickhandles the puck through the Rangers' defense.*

50-goal and 213 100-point seasons recorded in the NHL, and only 32 60-or-more goal performances and 42 130-point seasons registered. Of these totals, the Great One has had 9 50-goal seasons; five times he has scored 60 goals or better; he has broken the 100-point mark 14 times; and has scored over 130 points in all but one of his NHL seasons. In March of 1994, Gretzky eclipsed Gordie Howe as the highest goal-scorer of all time in the NHL, breaking Howe's lifetime mark of 801 goals. The leap in scoring output Gretzky has engineered appears absurd when measured against the performance standards of other sports. It is analogous to a track star suddenly running a consistent 2:30 mile, race after race. Or a golfer always hitting the green with his drive and then usually one-putting. In comparison, even the best of the other athletes suddenly look ordinary.

Sportswriters and theoreticians have spent hours and hours

trying to answer the question, 'How does Wayne Gretzky do it?' The answer lies in a complex combination of skills and happenstance.

Gretzky was born into a family that didn't reject as outrageous the notion that their six-year-old son could be the best hockey player in the world if he worked hard enough perfecting his skills. Gretzky himself was blessed with the patience to put in the work, as well as the reflexes, flexibility and intelligence to become the best. Gordie Howe, himself a candidate for best-ever hockey player, says, 'The more you watch

him play, and the more you know about hockey, the better you realize he is.'

Glen Sather, the coach, general manager and president of the Oilers, built a free-wheeling club that could derive greatest benefits from Gretzky's talents. Glenn Anderson, Jari Kurri and Mark Messier were offensive stars that every team's general manager coveted. Andy Moog and Grant Fuhr were among the best contemporary goaltenders and Paul Coffey was the first defenseman to be near the top of the scoring race since Bobby Orr. The Oilers broke all single-season team scoring records,

scoring more than 400 goals per season for five straight years, beginning in 1981/82.

The Oilers reached the playoffs in their first year in the NHL. In 1980/81, they shocked Montreal with a three-game sweep of the Canadiens in the preliminary round. In 1982/83, they reached the Stanley Cup finals, losing to the Islanders in four straight games, but the following year, 1983/84, they dethroned the Islanders and captured the Stanley Cup in five games. Edmonton made it a double the following year, needing just five games to defeat Philadelphia in the finals.

ABOVE LEFT: *Paul Coffey was only the third defenseman ever to score 100 points in a season.*

ABOVE: *Glen Sather served as coach, general manager and president of the Edmonton Oilers, and led them to five Stanley Cups.*

A Question of Balance

Amid much talk of dynasty, the 1985/86 Oilers set out in pursuit of their third straight Cup, but an inspired performance by their provincial rivals, the Calgary Flames, eliminated the Oilers in a thrilling seven-game Smythe Division final. Calgary then went on to defeat St Louis in another seven-game encounter before finally succumbing to a rookie-laden Montreal Canadiens team in the Stanley Cup finals.

The 1985/86 Canadiens were a team in transition, trying to work as many as 10 promising newcomers into their lineup in the course of the season. After an 87-point regular season, Montreal clicked in the playoffs, getting magnificent goaltending from rookie Patrick Roy and strong performances from their entire lineup. Veterans Larry Robinson, Bob Gainey, Guy Carbonneau, Bobby Smith and Mats Naslund were joined by such young players as Claude Lemieux, Brian Skrudland, Kjell Dahlin and David Maley to produce the victory and return Montreal to the elite tier of NHL clubs.

Edmonton, with Gretzky, remained the favorite to win the Cup over the next few seasons, but the NHL in the late 1980s was a balanced competition. Philadelphia, Washington, Montreal, Quebec and Calgary became potential winners, once the issue of stopping Gretzky and the Oilers had been dealt with. Calgary accomplished this feat in 1985/86, but only by the slimmest of margins – a one-goal victory in a seventh game that featured a goal scored by an Edmonton player into his own net. Many other clubs were only a notch or two away from contending and began improving rapidly. Included in this group were Hartford, New Jersey, Toronto, St Louis and Pittsburgh. It became a time of approaching parity and growing rivalries throughout the NHL.

The 1987 Stanley Cup playoffs produced some of the finest and most competitive hockey of the decade, culminating in the first seven-game series since Montreal defeated Chicago back in 1971. Among the many outstanding performances that highlighted the 1986/87 playoff year, none was more exciting or memorable than Game Seven of the Washington-NY Islander semi-final. It took over six periods to decide this one, but the Isles triumphed behind Kelly Hrudey's 73 saves and Pat LaFontaine's winning marker at 68:47 of overtime.

The Division finals proved equally entertaining, with three of the four series going the distance. Philadelphia and Montreal escaped from the Wales Conference, while Edmonton and Detroit proved best in the Campbell. The Conference finals, though well played and studded with one-goal victories, could not match the histrionics of the previous confrontations. Philadelphia squeezed by Montreal in six games, while Edmonton swept by Detroit in four straight, setting up a Stanley Cup final between these teams, both of whom have had their names engraved on the Cup twice. Luckily for fans worldwide, this series did not disappoint; it featured numerous come-from-behind victories by both squads. The Oilers were heavy favorites, but the Flyers surprised fans and experts alike. Anchored by the goaltending heroics of Ron Hextall (the eventual Conn Smythe winner) and the superb defensive play of Mark Howe, the Flyers forced the series to a seventh game before the Oilers pulled away to win their third Cup in four years.

Canada went through the round-robin set of games undefeated, tying both the powerful CSSR (Czechoslovakia) and USSR (Soviet Union) teams and ending up in first place. The USSR, Sweden and the Czechs finished behind the Canadians, setting up a Canada-CSSR semi-final, won by Team Canada 5-3. The other semi-final saw the USSR defeat the Swedes 4-2, avenging an earlier loss in the tournament. This set up the ultimate Canada-USSR confrontation – an unforgettable contest that surpassed even the super series of 1972 for intensity and enjoyment. All three games were decided by the same 6-5 score, two of them in overtime. The Canadians fashioned a comeback not unlike that of 1972: after losing game one in overtime, they withstood a determined Soviet effort to win game two in dramatic fashion, with Mario Lemieux climaxing 90 minutes of nail-biting drama with his overtime marker. This set the stage for game three, a match that exceeded all expectations to produce a superlative level of play.

The USSR, led by Fetisov, Makarov and Krutov, burst out of the blocks with a 3-0 lead after only 8 minutes of play. The Canadians gradually regained their composure and surged to attack, taking a 5-4 lead before the third period. The Soviets showed equal determination, and tied the score at 5s midway through the frame. The Canadians pressed for the winner, but were constantly thwarted by the goaltending of Mylinikov. With just over a minute remaining, Wayne Gretzky broke into the USSR zone and slipped a pass to an onrushing Lemieux, who fired the puck into the top shelf of the Soviet cage, thus

LEFT: *Mats Naslund in action during the playoffs with Hartford in 1985/86.*

LEFT: *Mario Lemieux in action in the 1987 Canada Cup tournament.*
RIGHT: *Team Canada celebrates its third Canada Cup victory.*

As thrilling as the playoffs were, they couldn't match the overwhelming response aroused by the Canada Cup series, held in September 1987. The previous Canada Cup events had produced terrific hockey, but no one was prepared for the intensity exhibited by the six combatants who took to the ice that fall. Canada, Finland, the United States, Sweden, Czechoslovakia and the Soviet Union prepared teams for this showdown that many will remember as the Series of the Century. The early round was loudly applauded for the quality of play, much of it without the rough stick work so common in the NHL. This was all the more remarkable, considering the European teams had numerous NHLers on the rosters.

cementing Canada's third Canada Cup victory.

This victory by Team Canada seemed to spark the country's other national squads, resulting in splendid performances in the Spengler Cup and Izvestia tournaments. The Canadian Olympic team, established four years earlier, surprised the hockey world with a victory in the Izvestia tournament. The Canadian team upset the USSR national team (the same squad that had lost in the Canada Cup finals) and captured the title. At the same time, another group of Canadians were winning the Spengler Cup for the second year in succession. This team, made up of ex-collegians and minor-leaguers, gave Canada its third world championship in four months. Add to this a champions banner for the Canadian Juniors, and the stage was set for the 1988 Winter Olympics.

For the first time in history, Canada was host to the Winter Olympics, which were held in Calgary, Alberta, during the month of February. Also for the first time, NHL players were allowed to compete in Olympic hockey, fueling hopes that Canada's 20-year drought as a medalist in ice hockey would come to an end. Team Canada was made up of college players, minor-leaguers and a handful of NHLers, including Ken Yaremchuk, Jim Peplinski and Andy Moog. The Izvestia triumph coupled with the team's extensive training schedule gave this group of youngsters great hope.

The hockey competition was full of surprises, but not, unfortunately, in Canada's favor. There were fine performances by the Swiss and Polish teams, a second-place silver medal for Finland (who defeated both Canada and the Soviet Union), and a disappointing display by the Czechs. The USSR played up to its full potential, winning the gold medal easily and regaining its status as the dominant international team. The Canadians

played well, but finished out of the medals, ending up in fourth place. Despite this, a number of Canadian team members have since made an early mark in the NHL — Sean Burke, Bob Joyce, Trent Yawney and Craig Janney, among others, have shown great promise.

Of special note were the many players for European squads who had been tutored in Canada and went on to play key roles overseas. Both the West German and French teams had numerous Canadian players on their rosters.

Hockey Hall of Fame inductees for 1987 included defensemen Jacques Lapierre and Leo Boivin. Ed Giacomin and Bobby Clarke also entered the home of hockey immortals — a just reward for their years of outstanding service. NHL president John Ziegler was inducted in the 1987 ceremony, in recognition of his guidance in the executive ranks.

The 1988 Stanley Cup playoffs seemed destined to produce a new champion. Throughout the 1987/88 regular season, Calgary and Montreal were the top teams, while the Flames had the edge on their division rivals, the Edmonton Oilers. But

RIGHT: *Lanny McDonald holds aloft the Stanley Cup after the Calgary Flames took it from the Montreal Canadiens in 1989. The triumph marked the end of McDonald's outstanding career.*

BELOW RIGHT: *Doug Gilmour goes after the Canadiens' Chris Chelios in the 1989 Cup finals.*

LEFT: *Steve Smith of the Oilers and Ray Bourque of the Boston Bruins during the 1988 Stanley Cup finals.*

the Oilers' star players – Gretzky, Kurri, Messier and Fuhr – saved their best performance for the playoffs, stunning Calgary with a four-game sweep in the Smythe Division final.

In the Adams Division, Boston won by upsetting Montreal, four games to one. The Bruins hadn't beaten the Canadiens in a playoff round since 1943. Boston received splendid goaltending from Rejean Lemelin and great play from such players as captain Ray Bourque and forwards Cam Neely, Craig Janney and Bob Joyce.

The New Jersey Devils – who qualified for the playoffs with an overtime goal on the last day of the regular season – defeated the Islanders and Capitals to advance to the NHL's final four. Goaltender Sean Burke from the Canadian Olympic team gave the young Devils spectacular netminding and made them into the Cinderella team of 1988.

Under coach Jacques Demers the Detroit Red Wings continued to dominate the Norris Division. En route to a second consecutive division title, they defeated Toronto and St Louis. The Wings were the only one of the NHL's four division winners of the regular season to survive the first two rounds of the playoffs. Flashy Czech scorer Petr Klima had a hat trick in both series.

In a replay of 1987, Edmonton needed five games to eliminate Detroit and win the Campbell Conference championship. In this playoff, the Oilers' savvy was increasingly apparent, as Gretzky controlled the tempo of each game with a flair matching that of Bobby Orr in the early 1970s.

The Bruins earned their first trip to the finals since 1978 by defeating the Devils in a seven-game series. The fourth game (which was won by New Jersey, 3-1) was officiated by an amateur referee and linesman, because the regular NHL officials were protesting the presence of coach Jim Schoenfeld behind the New Jersey bench. Schoenfeld had received a one-game suspension from the NHL for verbally abusing a referee after game three. Schoenfeld went on to serve his suspension later in the series.

Edmonton entered the Stanley Cup finals as the favorite over

the Bruins. A sweep seemed inevitable after Edmonton won the first three games. But in the second period of game four when the Oilers had just scored the tying goal the lights went out in Boston Garden. Unfortunately, the antiquated arena's lack of reliable auxiliary power forced the suspension of the game. Consequently, the remainder of the series was played in the arena at Edmonton where the Oilers clinched their fourth Stanley Cup in five seasons with a 6-3 victory.

In the 1987/88 season, the Oilers' Wayne Gretzky again demonstrated that he was the world's greatest hockey player. In the finals Gretzky scored the Cup-winning goal, and his 13 points posted a new NHL record. Moreover, for the playoffs, Gretzky won the Conn Smythe Trophy as MVP and was the top scorer with 43 points.

The hockey world went into shock when on 8 August 1988, Oilers' owner Peter Pocklington and General Manager Glen Sather announced they had sold Wayne Gretzky to the Los Angeles Kings. The Oilers would survive the trauma, but they would never be the same again.

In another surprising move, former Canadiens' superstar and Hall of Famer Guy Lafleur announced that he was planning a comeback with the New York Rangers. In the 1988/89 season, he displayed the form that had made him one of the league's foremost entertainers, compiling 45 points in limited action. The highlight of Lafleur's season was his return to the Montreal Forum, where he scored a pair of goals, helping the Rangers slip past the Habs.

For the first time in many years, the playoff race appeared to be wide open. As the 1988/89 NHL postseason wound up to the crescendo, only two teams were left standing. The Montreal-Calgary final was a rematch of the 1986 series, but this time the Flames' firepower overwhelmed the defense-minded Habs and they slipped past Montreal in six close games. The decisive sixth match was played at the Montreal Forum and marked the first time that the Canadiens lost the Cup on home ice. The championship final also was the end of Lanny McDonald's distinguished career.

The Great Gretzky Sale and the Oilers' Bust

On 26 May 1988, the Edmonton Oilers took possession of the Stanley Cup for the fourth time. After the traditional on-ice Cup parade, captain Wayne Gretzky whistled his fellow champions to center ice for an impromptu team photo. The heroes, many of whom had skated with the club on their three previous triumphs, were all there: Jari Kurri, Mark Messier, Glenn Anderson, Kevin Lowe, and of course, Wayne Gretzky himself. It would be the last time this talented group of athletes would play together as Edmonton Oilers.

Wayne Gretzky spent a lot of time in the public eye in 1988. The Stanley Cup parade was followed by his very public wedding to Hollywood starlet Janet Jones. Before the summer was over, he was to be the center of national attention again. Early in August, the rumor mill was at full tilt. Fax machines and phone lines burned late into the night with speculation that something was up, and it concerned Wayne Gretzky. He was going to Vancouver, to Detroit, even to Toronto. The truth of the matter was that there was news to be had, but it was already old news: Gretzky had been a Los Angeles King since late July. Oilers' owner Peter Pocklington needed money more than he needed another Stanley Cup miniature for his mantle. His player portfolio bulged with blue chip assets, and some of them knew they were going to be cashed in. In retrospect, the sale of Wayne Gretzky, the most valuable commodity on ice, should have been predictable, but when the world woke up to the announcement on 9 August 1988, the Great Gretzky Sale put a nation into shock.

The rumors began almost before the 1988 Stanley Cup

champagne was poured. Early in the summer, the word came down that he was to be sold. The deal seems to have been that Pocklington would give Gretzky a choice in his destination, and in return, the Great One would go quietly. Only six days following his wedding, Gretzky entered into discussions with Los Angeles Kings' owner Bruce McNall, a collector of fine art, ancient coins, winning thoroughbreds, and very soon, some of the world's best athletes. Gretzky, Pocklington and McNall agreed on money and terms that gave everyone what they needed, including time to prepare for the onslaught of public hewing and gnashing of teeth. Nobody expected Edmontonians, or Canadians across the land, to take the news without a national bally-hoo. But they didn't expect the level of public bad will that the sale brought down on Peter Pocklington and Janet Gretzky. She was seen as the 'Yoko Ono' of the hockey world, while Peter Puck came off like cartoon villain Snideley Whiplash, twirling mustaches and making an orphan of the country's native son.

In time, the details of the deal surfaced. Gretzky and teammates Marty McSorley and Mike Krushelnyski went south to the City of Angels, for Jimmy Carson, Martin Gelinas, three first-round draft choices, and $15 million in cash.

With the sale of Gretzky, a chapter in the history of the game had come to a close. Without Gretzky, the Oilers were demoralized. They played the 1988/89 season as if in a state of shock. The team struggled to a third place finish and, adding insult to injury, were ousted from the first round of the playoffs by none other than the Great One and his new royal entourage.

The Oilers had not won four Stanley Cups on the strength of one player, however. The team had a strong nucleus, and was managed by one of the best in the business. In 1990, a new leader emerged from the pack and brought them back into the winner's circle: Mark Messier assumed Gretzky's captainship and on-ice leadership, finishing second in the scoring race and winning the Hart Trophy as the league's MVP for the 1989/90 season. With Bill Ranford in net, replacing the injured Grant Fuhr, the Oilers were strong throughout the playoffs, losing only six games and proving to the world that they could win the Stanley Cup without Wayne Gretzky.

Losing Wayne Gretzky was the end of a chapter for the Edmonton Oilers, but by the early 1990s, they closed the book on the 'dynasty that was.' Mark Messier, Esa Tikkanen and Kevin Lowe took their show to Broadway, playing with the Rangers; Grant Fuhr and Glenn Anderson helped revitalize the Toronto Maple Leafs; Steve Smith solidified the blue line in Chicago; Jari Kurri and Charlie Huddy joined the King in Hollywood; and Craig Simpson shuffled off to Buffalo. The last player remaining was the man they said had the hardest head in hockey: Craig MacTavish, the last player to play pro hockey without a helmet, stayed on to carry the torch for a dynasty team still regaled in the taverns of Edmonton. In 1992/93 the Edmonton Oilers missed the playoffs for the first time in team history. The team that had once scored 400 goals five years in a row put up only 242 goals on the scoreboard for the 1992/93 campaign. Early in 1993/94, Glen Sather replaced Ted Green behind the Oilers' bench, hoping for a bestseller in the sequel to the 'Champions of the Northlands.'

ABOVE: *Gretzky displays his new team jersey at a 1988 press conference.*
BELOW LEFT: *Team captain Wayne Gretzky gathers his troops for an on-ice photograph following the Oilers' 1988 Stanley Cup victory over the Boston Bruins. It would be his last performance in an Oilers' uniform.*

RIGHT: *Doug Weight joined the Oilers from the Rangers in the 1992/93 season and led the Oilers in scoring four times, including a career-high 104 points during the 1995/96 season.*

The Russians Are Coming

In the 1950s, the Russians took their new hockey skills into international competition, and almost from the first, dominated European, World and Olympic play. Their rigorous training and game rehearsals were legendary in the hockey world, and were judged, by the Russians, to be the better system of playing hockey. The peculiarities of conflicting playing seasons and the icy political climate kept the best Russian players from ever meeting a top-ranked North American team. In 1972, when some of the sting had gone out of the international frostbite, the Soviet National Hockey Team faced a who's who All Star Team from Canada in an eight-game summit: The Series of the Century. Canada narrowly defeated the Soviets 4-3-1, with the winning goal being scored with only 34 seconds remaining in the eighth, decisive game. For the rest of the decade, club teams from the Soviet Union barnstormed North American hockey towns, playing NHL, WHA and minor league teams from Portland, Oregon, to Portland, Maine.

Although by the late 1970s players from numerous Eastern European countries had signed NHL contracts, no Soviet-trained player had made the jump to the NHL. In 1983, the Los Angeles Kings shocked the hockey world by signing little-known Soviet star Victor Nechaev. Nechaev had married an American nurse and gone West with her. The Kings signed him to a three-game trial, and although he scored a goal in his trio of games, he was released, refusing to report to the minors.

The political climate between East and West warmed considerably in the 1980s, and for the past ten years, NHL teams had been selecting Russian players in the annual Amateur/Entry drafts. The Soviet Ice Hockey Federation and the NHL finally hammered out a financial package that strengthened the Russian ice hockey machine, in exchange for recognizing NHL contracts with Russian players. Late in 1989, the first Soviet-trained player made his debut in the NHL. Sergei Priakin, a 12th-round draft choice of the Calgary Flames, joined the team for the last two games of the schedule. In 1990, some of the biggest names in Russian hockey pulled on NHL jerseys, including the KLM line: Victor Krutov, Igor Larianov and Sergei Makarov. Others included Viacheslav Fetisov, Sergei Starikov and Helmut Balderis, who played for Team Russia in the 1976 Canada Cup tournament. Sergei Makarov

LEFT: *Sergei Priakin (center), the first Soviet-trained player in the NHL, in action with the Calgary Flames in 1991.*

became the first Russian player to win a major NHL award, bringing home the Calder Trophy as the league's best rookie. But the public outcry that a player who had spent 13 seasons with the Soviet National Team could still be considered a rookie was so great that the NHL changed the rules concerning the award: no player over the age of 26 would be eligible to win the rookie prize.

By the early 1990s, every NHL team would have at least one Soviet-born player on its roster, and it wasn't long before some became NHL superstars. Pavel Bure, the league's best freshman in 1991/92, became the first Vancouver Canuck to score 50 goals in a season, collecting 60 goals and 100 points to lead the team. In 1992/93, Buffalo's Alexander Mogilny became the first Soviet player to lead the league in goals, connecting 76 times to tie for the league lead with the 'Finnish Flash', Teemu Selanne. Detroit's Sergei Fedorov is another Russian superstar. One of the finest two-way players in the game and a two-time recipient of the Selke Trophy as the NHL's top defensive forward, Fedorov has recorded 871 points in his 12-year career with Detroit.

Young talent continues to arrive from small towns across the biggest stretch of hockey country in the world. From Siberia to the Bering Strait, from Moscow to Leningrad, children of all ages are playing hockey with dreams of joining their brothers from Moose Jaw, Saskatchewan, and Hibbing, Minnesota, in the world's greatest professional hockey league, the NHL.

TOP RIGHT: *Buffalo Sabres star Alexander Mogilny was the first Soviet player to lead the league in goals.*

RIGHT: *Known as the 'Russian Rocket', Pavel Bure is one of only two players (Teemu Selanne is the other) to record two 50-goal seasons with two different teams.*

Mario and Eric

The first half of the 1980s were dominated by a skinny finesse player from Brantford, Ontario. Wayne Gretzky set standards of excellence that may never be surpassed. When he first entered the league in 1979, the word on the street was that he was just too small to make it in the big league. By 1984, they were serving crow as an entrée in press boxes from New York to LA. Scouts around the NHL scoured the junior leagues and American universities in hopes of finding another 'one.'

They found him in Laval, Quebec, and he was bigger and stronger than Gretzky. No one had dominated the Quebec Junior Hockey League like Mario Lemieux. He eradicated all of Guy Lafleur's and Mike Bossy's records, and was the most touted prospect since the Great One himself. In his final year as a junior, Lemieux scored 133 goals and set up 149 more for an incredible 282 points. It was obvious that Lemieux would be the top choice in the 1984 entry draft. NHL officials watched in horror as the Pittsburgh Penguins and the New Jersey Devils staged a battle for the basement, displaying some of the most lackluster hockey since the Pittsburgh Pirates played hockey in the mid-1920s.

Pittsburgh had the dubious honor of finishing in last place, giving them the biggest prize in hockey since the Montreal Canadiens hoodwinked the California Seals into trading their 1971 first round draft choice, which turned out to be the number one pick of the season, Guy Lafleur. Lemieux demonstrated all of Gretzky's skills. He was a wizard with the wand, and what he lacked in pure hockey sense he made up for in brawn. In his first shift of his first NHL game, he stole the puck from All-Star Ray Bourque, romped in on a breakaway, and scored. On his next shift, he showed that he had it where Gretzky did not: Lemieux was not to be trifled with. He left his gloves on the ice and rumbled with the Boston defence.

Lemieux was a runaway winner of the Calder Trophy as rookie of the year in 1985, collecting an even 100 points and

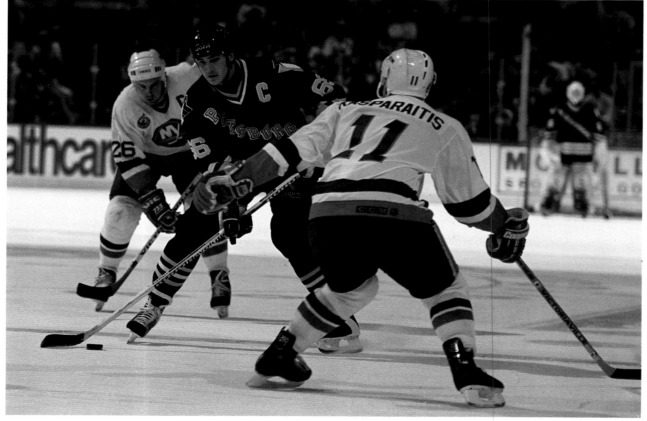

TOP LEFT: *Super Mario Lemieux instantly joined the ranks of hockey's greatest in his rookie season with the Pittsburgh Penguins.*
LEFT: *Lemieux's combination of skill and brawn makes him a formidable opponent.*

ABOVE RIGHT: *Lemieux steals the puck during game four of the 1992 Stanley Cup playoffs.*

improving the standard of play in Pittsburgh. The Penguins were better, but it was a long way from the cellar to the playoffs. As good as he was, it takes more than one superstar to win a Stanley Cup, and the Pittsburgh front office slowly built a team around Super Mario.

In 1988 Lemieux won his first Art Ross Trophy, scoring 70 goals and 168 points. The following year he became the first player since Phil Esposito in 1973 to lead the league in goals (85), assists (114) and points (199). He also became the first player since Gordie Howe to lead the league in scoring while spending 100 minutes in the penalty box. Lemieux took special pride in winning the Hart Trophy, becoming the first player not named Gretzky to win the award in the 1980s.

By 1991, the Pittsburgh Penguins were among the finest squads in the NHL loop. Although Lemieux missed most of the season with a back injury, he worked himself into shape for the playoffs and led the Penguins to their first Stanley Cup title, collecting 44 points in 23 postseason games. Injuries continued to plague the big centerman in 1992, and although he missed 16 games, he still led the league with 131 points. The Penguins waddled their way into the playoffs, and left behind all detractors, tying an NHL record with 10 consecutive playoff victories, and winning the Cup. Super Mario scored 16 goals in 15 games, and became the first player since Bernie Parent to win back-to-back Conn Smythe trophies.

Through much of his career, Lemieux has been plagued by injury. Unlike Gretzky, he plays the corners, and stands his ground in the slot. Injuries are part of the game, but what ended Mario Lemieux's season in 1992/93 was not expected. In January he was diagnosed with Hodgkins disease, a dangerous but treatable form of cancer. Lemieux was out of the Pittsburgh lineup for eight weeks, undergoing chemotherapy. No one expected him to return that season. Many didn't expect him to return at all. But when the call came for the Penguins to make a run for the playoffs, big Number 66 answered the whistle. After losing their first game with Lemieux back in the lineup, the Penguins went on a record roll, winning their final 17 games of the season. Although the Penguins headed for the golf course after the second round of playoffs, no one would dare deny that Mario Lemieux was one of the finest men ever to play the game.

With Gretzky and Lemieux hogging most of the ink in The Hockey News, the search was on for 'The Next One.' He was found in one of hockey's richest talent mines: St Michael's Collegiate in central Toronto, a school that produced such Hall of Famers as Frank Mahovlich, Dave Keon and Red Kelly. Eric Lindros made it to the NHL in 1992, but he took one of the most circuitous and controversial routes in the history of the game. Lindros carries some revolutionary ideas in his equipment bag. He believes that an athlete should have some say in where

he plays his game. In the end, Lindros has had his way, and has maybe broken some ground for the 'next ones.'

Like Gretzky before him, Lindros was a media darling as a young player. When the Sault Ste Marie Greyhounds chose him as the number one pick in the junior draft, Lindros refused to report, insisting that he wanted to remain close to Toronto, where he intended to continue his education. He joined the Detroit Compuware of the USHL, where he collected 52 points in only 14 games. The Greyhounds then traded Lindros' rights to the Oshawa Generals and Lindros suited up for the suburban Toronto team. In 1990/91, after leading the OHL in points, Lindros helped the Generals win the Memorial Cup for the North American junior hockey championship.

The Quebec Nordiques, who finished last in the NHL in the 1991 season, had the first overall selection in the NHL draft, and it was clear that Lindros would get the nod. However, Lindros informed the team that he had no intention of playing hockey in Quebec City, and would rather sit out the two-year period than play in a 'small market' hockey town. The uproar in Quebec rivaled the 'Richard Riot' of 1955 in emotion, if not in actions, but Lindros remained adamant. When the Nordiques made him their number one choice, he refused to report to training camp, or even to negotiate the terms of a $50 million, ten-year contract. Instead, he became the first non-professional to play for Team Canada in the Canada Cup tournament. As fate would have it, one of his first games with Team Canada was in Quebec City, and he answered his critics by scoring his first goal in that NHL arena. Later that season, he suited up with the Canadian National and Canadian

Olympics teams, helping Canada win its first Olympic medal since 1968. In June of 1992, convinced finally that the big Anglophone would never play in Quebec, the Nordiques traded his rights to the Philadelphia Flyers.

The Flyers, one of the most respected hockey organizations in the league, had fallen on hard times. They needed another star with Bobby Clarke-like qualities to rekindle the fire of earlier days. They traded six players, two first-round draft choices, and $15 million in cash to get the man they hoped would bring glory back to Broad Street.

At 6 feet 4 inches and 235 pounds, Lindros is an imposing figure at center. He shows natural leadership qualities, has a reach that rivals any man in the game, and delivers punishing body checks to anyone in his way. He can also do what a great centerman is paid to do: he scores goals. In his rookie season, he collected 75 points in 61 games and appeared a natural to win the Calder Trophy until a knee injury ended his season. Although the Flyers gave up a lot to get him, they had their finest season since 1989.

Although Lindros had the ability to inspire those who played with him to perform beyond their natural abilities, his stay in Philadelphia was marked by controversy, disappointment and injury. Lindros was named the NHL's MVP in the strike-shortened 1994/95 season and was a pivotal factor in guiding the Flyers to the Stanley Cup finals in 1996/97. In the years that followed, the Big E became a victim of his own rambunctious style. Lindros suffered numerous injuries, including a series of concussions that threatened to end his career. He was also involved in a heated war of words with Flyers general manager Bobby Clarke over his contract status and a number of comments made by the Lindros camp concerning his treatment by the Philadelphia medical staff while he was recovering from his head injuries. Forced to sit out the entire 2000/01 season, Lindros was finally traded to the NY Rangers prior to the 2001/02 season.

LEFT: *Mario Lemieux shows off his prize after leading the Penguins to their second consecutive Stanley Cup victory, in 1992.*

BELOW: *Although he missed 23 games due to injury in the 1992/93 season, Eric Lindros set a rookie record for the Philadelphia Flyers with 41 goals that season.*

Into the 1990s

The 1990s were heralded by a season marked by close competition. An average of only 16 points stood between first and fourth place in the league's four divisions for the 1989/90 season, with only the Boston Bruins, coached by former defenceman Mike Milbury, hitting the triple-figure mark in points. They went on to meet the Gretzkyless Edmonton Oilers in the finals.

Meanwhile, in Los Angeles, Gretzky was busy breaking a new record. At the start of the season, Gretzky was only 14 points away from surpassing Gordie Howe as the league's all-time scoring leader. On 15 October, ironically in a game against the Oilers, Gretzky recorded career point number 1851 to drop Gordie Howe, Mr Hockey himself, into second place on the NHL's all-time points leader board.

In the Stanley Cup finals, the first game required three overtime periods to resolve a 2-2 tie. Edmonton's Petr Klima made a rare overtime appearance in the third extra session and pointed a slapshot between Andy Moog's legs to give the Oilers a 3-2 victory and a series lead they would never give up. The Oilers wrapped up the postseason, and their fifth Stanley Cup, in five uneven games, outscoring Boston 20-6 without the help of Wayne Gretzky. Oilers' second string goaltender Bill Ranford, who had taken over for the injured Grant Fuhr and done a splendid job, was the Conn Smythe Trophy winner.

In the 1990/91 season, the Toronto Maple Leafs franchise continued its decline into the doldrums. The Leafs, once one of the league's most respected organizations, were a complete disaster during the 1990/91 campaign. The last quarter century had seen them struggle to compete, but with the death of long-time owner and curmudgeon Harold Ballard, the team was disorganized and unmotivated, and wound up in last place in the Norris Division.

With Mario Lemieux out of action for the lion's share of the season, Wayne Gretzky returned to the top in the scoring competition, with 163 points to lead all NHL scorers. Gretzky, the

league assists leader for 12 consecutive seasons, became the first player in the history of the game to reach the 2000 point mark.

The postseason was full of surprises. The contenders, Pittsburgh and Minnesota, had both missed the playoffs the previous season, and this year found themselves in the Stanley Cup finals. Never before had the fortunes of the league changed so radically over the course of a single season. Pittsburgh, with a healthy Mario Lemieux leading the way, skated past New Jersey, Washington and Boston to reach the final for the first time in franchise history. The Minnesota North Stars,

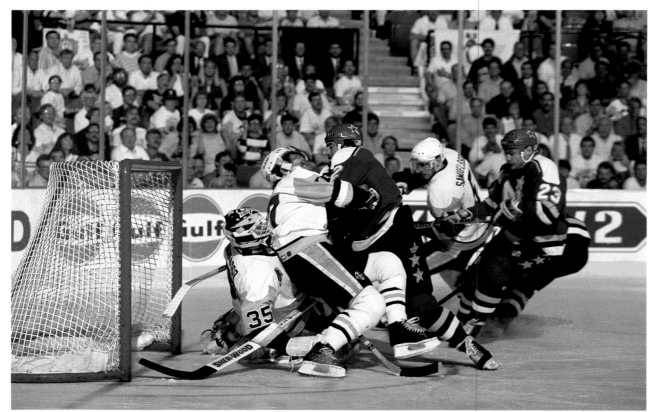

ABOVE: *In his second season with the Los Angeles Kings, Wayne Gretzky broke Gordie Howe's record for most goals in an NHL career.*
LEFT: *Paul Coffey (77) loses his helmet as he helps Tom Barrasso (35) at the goal line in 1991 Stanley Cup action.*

RIGHT: *Eric Lindros played for Team Canada in the 1991 Canada Cup tournament while he held out from playing with the Quebec Nordiques, who had made him the first pick in the 1991 draft.*

who finished well below .500 in the regular season (27-39-14) downed Chicago, St Louis and Edmonton to earn a Stanley Cup final tilt with Pittsburgh. The series is remembered as a first in three categories. It was the first time two teams who had missed the previous playoffs met in the finals, the first time that two post-1967 expansion teams played for the Cup, and the first time since 1936 that two teams who had never won the Cup met on Stanley Cup ice.

In the final, the superior potency of the Penguins' lineup wore down the overachieving North Stars. The Penguins had bench strength and confidence, and hung up the Stanley Cup banner after six games. The Penguins' Mario Lemieux, whose 44 postseason points was the second highest in postseason history, took home the Conn Smythe Trophy.

The 1991/92 season marked the 75th anniversary of the National Hockey League. On the opening night of the schedule, the original six teams paired off, each team facing their historical rivals. The teams wore replica uniforms, celebrating their own, and the league's, history. The Toronto-Montreal match was the premier event of the night, garnering the most media attention.

The 1991/92 season saw the NHL introduce a new franchise for the first time since 1979. The San Jose Sharks, who were owned by George and Gordon Gund, former owners of the North Stars, were to play in the Smythe Division. They had access to players from the Minnesota team, and were able to stock their tank from the unprotected pools around the league.

With only a few games left in the 1991/92 schedule, the NHL encountered the same sort of labor troubles that had befallen both major league baseball and pro football. On 1 April 1992, the NHL Players Association called the first league-wide strike in NHL history. League president John Ziegler and Players Association chief Bob Goodenow negotiated in private and bellowed at one another publicly for 10 days before a new deal was made. Soon after the conclusion of the playoffs, Ziegler was forced to resign, ending his 15-year tenure as NHL president. Gil Stein, the NHL's vice president and the league's general council, replaced him on an interim basis.

In the Stanley Cup finals, the Pittsburgh Penguins met the Chicago Black Hawks, who entered the finals riding a post-season record 11-game winning streak. In the series opener, the Hawks jumped to a 4-1 lead, only to see the Penguins battle back to win the match 5-4. The Penguins were on an eight-game unbeaten streak of their own, and were in full stride through the playoffs. They won the remaining three games, matching the Hawks' newly set record of 11 straight post-season wins and capturing their second consecutive Stanley Cup. The Penguins' margin of victory in the four-game sweep was five goals, the slimmest goal differential since Montreal defeated St Louis in 1968. Mario Lemieux led all playoff scorers with 34 points, becoming the second player ever (Bernie Parent was the first) to win back-to-back Conn Smythe trophies.

The summer of '92 was a time of change for the NHL. It was decided that a commissioner would be chosen to replace interim president Gil Stein, though what this meant to the power structure of the league was yet to be seen. National Basketball Association vice president Gary Bettman was hired for the new position, on the strength of his expertise in labor management and his marketing know-how.

Two new teams joined the NHL for the 1992/93 season. The Ottawa Senators were resurrected after almost 60 years, and

TOP RIGHT: *Mario Lemieux became only the second player ever to take home back-to-back Conn Smythe trophies, in 1991 and 1992.*

RIGHT: *Lemieux in action during game one of the 1992 Stanley Cup finals.*

The first woman ever to play on an NHL team, Rheaume got her first start in an exhibition game on 23 September 1992 against St Louis, allowing two goals in one period of work.

The Norris Division was once again one of the league's strongest, with a revitalized Toronto Maple Leafs franchise, coached by former Canadiens' leader Pat Burns, shaking up the loop. MVP candidate Doug Gilmour set club records for points and assists, and rookie goaltender Felix Potvin led the league in goals-against average. The Leafs made it back into playoff contention with a club record 99 points and a total of 44 victories.

The Minnesota North Stars, Cup finalists just two seasons before, played the season with a sense that change was in the air. Team owner Norman Green gave notice that he was looking for a new home for his franchise, and that he was looking south. The northern lights went dark as Green announced that he was taking his team to the Lone Star State for the 1993/94 season. As the Dallas Stars made their NHL debut, they heralded the end of a 26-year history in the Land of Lakes.

In the playoff round, the Los Angeles Kings defeated Calgary, Vancouver and Toronto to reach the Stanley Cup finals for the first time. They had their work cut out for them as they faced the Montreal Canadiens, who had disposed of Quebec, Buffalo and the New York Islanders in their quest for their 24th Stanley Cup. The Canadiens, who had won eight of the nine overtime matches in the preliminary rounds, disrobed the Kings in five games, including two more overtime victories to take home the Cup and solidify their place as sport's most winning organization.

When the curtain opened for the start of the 1993/94 season, the NHL had a much different look. The Mighty Ducks of Anaheim, California, and the Florida Panthers joined the loop, bringing the team count to 26. The Prince of Wales and Clarence Campbell conferences were renamed Eastern and Western, and the Adams, Patrick, Norris and Smythe divisions were simply called Northeast, Atlantic, Central and Pacific. There were various realignments to open the season, the most significant of which were Pittsburgh's departure from the competitive Atlantic Division to the Northeast, and Winnipeg's shift from the Pacific to the Central Division.

the Tampa Bay Lightning represented the league's first excursion into Florida. In a move which may signal the biggest change in the history of the game, Lightning's manager Phil Esposito signed a woman to an NHL contract. Manon Rheaume, a goaltender who helped lead Canada to the Women's World Championship in 1992, surprised everyone, including Esposito, by rising above her detractors and performing admirably under the pressure of big-league hockey.

ABOVE: *Adam Oates, traded by the St Louis Blues to the Boston Bruins in 1992, helped take the Bruins to the top of the Adams Division in 1992/93.*

RIGHT: *Patrick Roy in goal for the Montreal Canadiens in the 1993 finals. The Canadiens took the Cup in five games from the Los Angeles Kings, and Roy won his second Conn Smythe Trophy.*

As the 1993/94 NHL season approached, media moguls looked for stories in Chicago, Toronto and Los Angeles. In Chicago, Steve Larmer, who had never missed a game in his NHL career, was 81 games away from a new 'Ironman' record. He refused to report to training camp, demanding a trade. He missed the first two weeks of play before being traded to the Rangers in a three-way deal with Hartford. In Toronto, scribes waited to see whether the club had truly turned over a new Leaf. They had: The Maple Leafs opened the season with a league record 10 consecutive victories. In Los Angeles, the odds makers were taking bets on when The Great One would eclipse Mr. Hockey. On March 23, 1994, Wayne Gretzky became the all-time scoring leader with his 802nd regular season marker, leaving Gordie Howe's record 801 in his wake. Gretzky won his 10th scoring title, but his Los Angeles Kings became the first team since the Canadiens of 1970 to appear in the finals one year and miss the playoffs the next.

The New York Rangers finished first in wins (52), overall points (112), home winning percentage (.738), road wins (24) and powerplay efficiency (23 percent). The New Jersey Devils finished a close second behind the Rangers in the Atlantic Division, with Jacques Lemaire and Larry Robinson behind the bench. Rookie standout Martin Brodeur finished second in goals-against average, and took home the Calder Trophy for his efforts. Eric Lindros and the Philadelphia Flyers could not get off the ground, missing the playoffs for the fifth straight year.

In the Central Division, five of the six teams finished above .500, with Detroit leading the pack with 100 points. Winnipeg's Teemu Selanne suffered an Achilles tendon tear, and his Jets landed in the NHL basement with 57 points on the season.

Despite having Mario Lemieux in the lineup for only 22 games, Pittsburgh won the Northeast Division. Jaromir Jagr led the Penguins with 99 points on the season. In Buffalo, Dominic Hasek was having a dream season, becoming the first goalie since Bernie Parent to finish with a goals-against average below 2.00. Hasek, the Vezina Trophy winner for 1993/94, led all goaltenders with a 1.95 GAA, a save percentage of .930, and registered 7 shutouts.

The Pacific Division was won by the Calgary Flames, while in San Jose, new coach Kevin Constantine led the Sharks to an NHL record for single-season improvement, finishing in third place with 82 points, 58 points more than their 1992/93 totals. In Vancouver, Pavel Bure led the league in goals with 60 markers, giving notice that Vancouver was a force to reckon with in the Western Conference.

In the opening postseason round, Vancouver rebounded from a 3-1 series deficit against Calgary, winning the next three games in overtime. They needed only five games to send Dallas to the golf course, and five more to drop the Maple Leafs before waiting for the Eastern finals contender.

The Rangers swept the Islanders and outscored the Washington Capitals 42-15 before meeting the real competition from New Jersey. The Rangers-Devils battle raged over seven games, three going to double overtime. New Jersey tied the seventh game in the final seconds, but lost it in the second overtime period on a heartbreaker by Stephane Matteau. Matteau became the first Ranger to score two overtime goals in the same series since Pete Stemkowski did it in 1971.

The final series was a classic contest of East versus West.

ABOVE: *The Rangers' talented defenseman Brian Leetch, seen here in game six of the 1994 Stanley Cup finals, took home the Conn Smythe Trophy for his superb performance in the exciting seven-game series.*
LEFT: *(Left to right) Leetch, Vancouver Canucks star Pavel Bure, and the Rangers' outstanding goalie Mike Richter do battle at the goal line in game six of the 1994 finals.*

OPPOSITE: *Team captain Mark Messier is all smiles as he holds the Stanley Cup after the Rangers' 3-2 victory in game seven of the 1994 finals.*

The Rangers, who had not won the Stanley Cup in 54 years, faced Vancouver, whose last Cup win came in 1915. New York defeated Vancouver in three of the first four games, but the Canucks came storming back with 6-3 and 4-1 wins to tie the series. Since the league began its expansion program in 1968, there had been only two seven-game contests in the finals, the last in 1987.

It was fitting that Mark Messier, captain of the New York Rangers, should score the Cup-winning goal. Try as they might, Vancouver could not overcome the 3-2 deficit, and when the last whistle was sounded, Messier, the former Edmonton Oiler, became the first man in league history to captain a team to the Cup with two different teams. Brian Leetch became the second defenseman to lead in playoff scoring with 11 goals and 23 assists, and the first US-born player to win the Conn Smythe Trophy. On June 17th, 1.5 million people poured out onto Broadway to honor their first Stanley Cup champions in more than half a century.

New Moves in the Mid-1990s

The final five seasons of the 1990s were years most notable for economic upheaval, franchise movement and the emergence of European-trained players as the dominant offensive stars of the NHL game.

After the completion of the 1994 exhibition season, NHL owners decided to lock out their players, bringing the season to an abrupt halt and creating the first work stoppage because of labor unrest in the history of the league. It took three months and 468 missed games for the NHL and the Players Association to reach a new Bargaining Agreement.

When the players finally hit the ice, the league was forced to begin the aborted season without one of its marquee stars.

Pittsburgh's magnificent Mario Lemieux took a medical leave of absence to recover from the effects of his fight against non-Hodgkin's lymphoma. The Penguins were still able to occupy the top rung of the NHL's scoring ladder thanks to Jaromir Jagr, who became the first European-trained player to win the Art Ross Trophy with 32 goals and 70 points. The Big E, Eric Lindros, also made his presence felt both physically and statistically. Lindros crushed opponents with booming bodychecks and used an assortment of dazzling offensive moves to earn the Hart Trophy as the league's MVP. The top sniper in the league was Washington's Peter Bondra, who popped 34 pucks behind opposition goaltenders.

LEFT: *Eric Lindros was dubbed as the Flyers' 'Next One' until injuries and a bitter feud with general manager Bob Clarke drove him out of Philadelphia.*

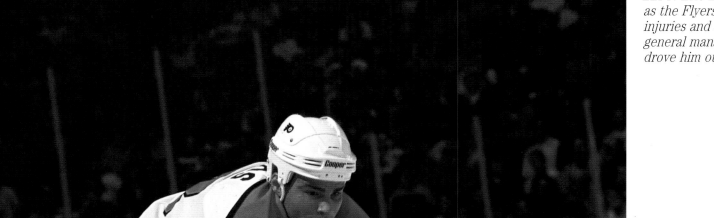

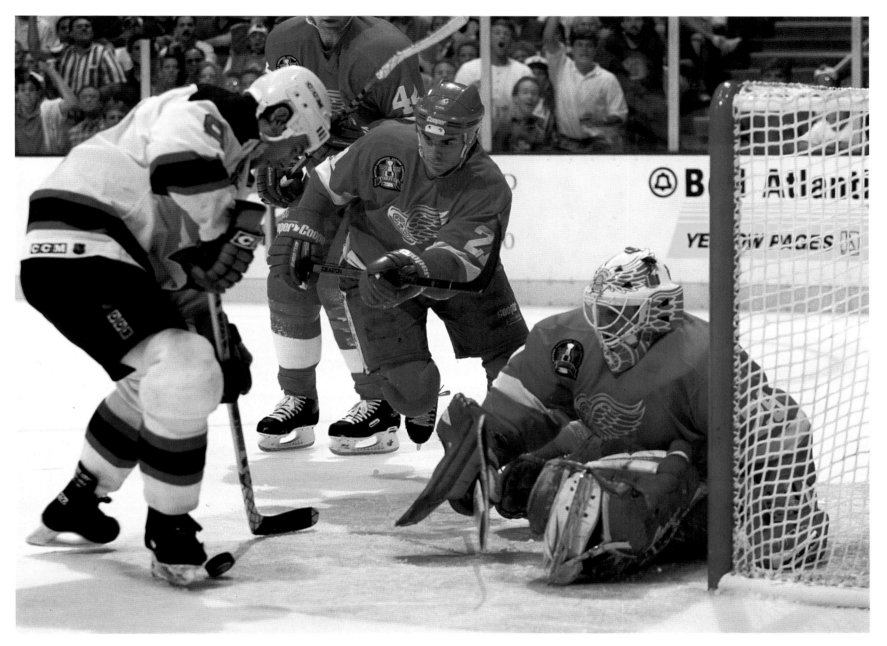

While much of the media's attention was focused on the health of Lemieux and the struggles of the defending Cup champion NY Rangers, the real story was emerging from the swamps of New Jersey. Under the direction of Jacques Lemaire, the Devils came within a double-overtime goal of reaching the finals in 1994. In 1994/95, Lemaire perfected a defensive system that became known as the neutral zone trap. It would become the most debated defensive maneuver in decades, and it would be instrumental in leading the Devils to their first Stanley Cup championship.

The Devils were a hardworking club with moderate offensive spark but blessed with gritty forwards, mobile defensemen and a blossoming superstar in goaltender Martin Brodeur. During the regular season, New Jersey finished only four games over .500. But Lemaire was grooming his team for playoff action, where checking was tight, scoring was light and fighting was slight.

New Jersey blanketed their opponents in the post-season with a smothering defensive style and an opportunistic offensive flair. The Devils lost only four games in the playoffs, calmly and confidently tearing apart their opposition with a fixated dedication to the defensive system Lemaire designed. In the finals against the powerhouse Detroit Red Wings, New Jersey's purposeful fore checking sunk the Motowners in four straight games, outscoring the Wings 16-7. Claude Lemieux, the 'Grate One', yapped and trapped throughout the entire playoffs, topping all post-season scorers with 13 goals to earn the Conn Smythe Trophy as the playoff MVP.

As the 1995/96 NHL season began, the league welcomed back a familiar face: Mario Lemieux returned to the game and proved he was not only recovered, he was rediscovered.

ABOVE: *Neal Broten (9) pops a rebound past the outstretched pad of Red Wings goaltender Mike Vernon during the New Jersey Devils' Stanley Cup-winning romp in 1995.*

The Magnificent One was purely marvelous, leading all scorers in goals (69), assists (92), points (161), power-play goals (31) and short-handed goals (8). The Penguins captain guided Pittsburgh to first place in the Northeast Division with 103 points.

Lemieux's remarkable comeback was certainly a key feature of the 1995/96 schedule, but the real headlines belonged to the province of Quebec. During the off-season, the Nordiques were sold to interests in Colorado, making the Nords the first of the WHA teams that joined the NHL in 1979/80 to relocate. They became the Colorado Avalanche.

The other major story line to emerge from La Belle Province concerned Montreal's eccentric goaltender, Patrick Roy. The Canadiens, who had failed to make the playoffs the previous year, started the 1995/96 season with five straight losses. In a shocking personnel move, the Habs fired both general manager Serge Savard and coach Jacques Demers, the duo who had guided Montreal to their 23rd Cup championship only two years earlier. Rejean Houle and Mario Tremblay were brought in as replacements, although neither of the former Habs stars had any coaching or managerial experience. One of the more vocal opponents of the changes was goaltender Patrick Roy, who was a staunch supporter of Serge Savard.

On Saturday, 2 December, in front of a nationwide television audience, Roy was blasted by the Detroit Red Wings, who were allowed to skate up and over the Habs and plant nine pucks behind the beleaguered netminder. Roy immediately demanded to be traded and two days later, he and team captain Mike Keane were dispatched to the newly transplanted Colorado Avalanche – an unthinkable transaction that would never have occurred six months earlier.

Over in California, the game's greatest player was tiring of the Hollywood spotlight. LA Kings captain Wayne Gretzky demanded to be traded, and his request was granted when the Kings sent the Great One to St Louis.

Amidst all the turmoil, a Cinderella story was being scripted in Florida. Copying the game plan of the 1995 champion New Jersey Devils, the Panthers featured tough defense, smart offense and overpowering special teams. With John Vanbiesbrouck supplying All-Star goaltending, Florida managed to make it all the way to the Stanley Cup finals.

Florida's opponents in the championship round were the Colorado Avalanche, who rode the brilliance of Patrick Roy's goaltending, the quiet leadership of Joe Sakic and the ferocious two-way play of Peter Forsberg all the way to the finals. They also had another sparkplug just waiting to add his name to the Stanley Cup record book in Claude Lemieux, the 1995 playoff MVP who was added to the Avalanche roster in the off-season.

The Avalanche needed six games in each series to reach the pinnacle of Cup success and once they got there, they were overpowering. The Panthers couldn't match the Avalanche's abundance of talent as Colorado clawed past the Panthers in four straight games. The finale of the series was a barn-burning, nail-biting 104-minute overtime marathon that wasn't decided until rearguard Uwe Krupp's blast from the blueline eluded Vanbiesbrouck to give Colorado a 1-0 victory and their first trip to the Stanley Cup winner's circle.

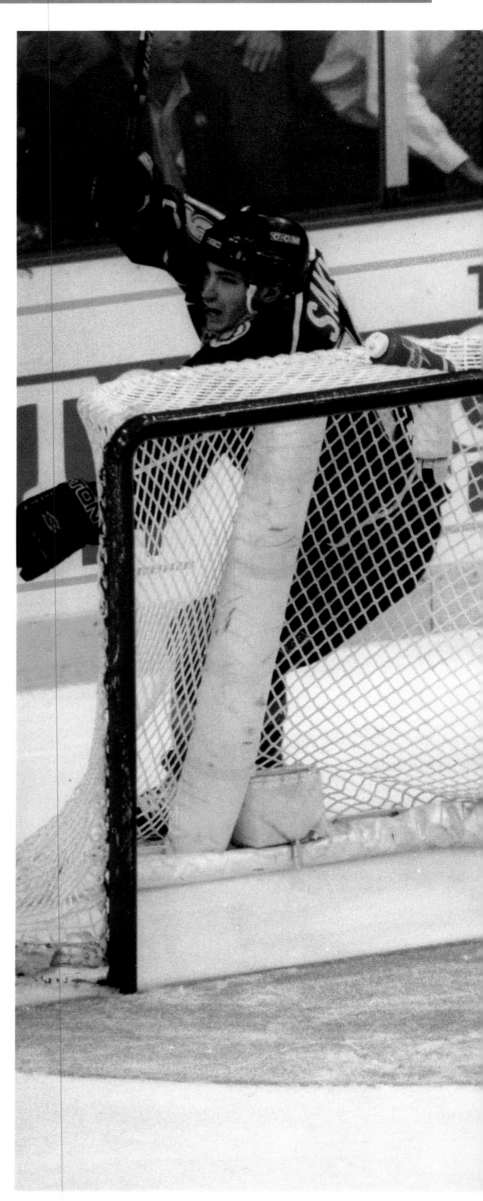

BELOW: 'Saint Patrick' Roy's stellar goaltending was a major factor in the Colorado Avalanche's Stanley Cup victory in 1995/96.

RIGHT: Florida netminder John Vanbiesbrouck can only look to the heavens after Uwe Krupp's blast from the blueline gave the Colorado Avalanche their first Stanley Cup championship.

The World Cup

Before the 1996/97 regular season opened, the inaugural World Cup of Hockey was held, featuring the eight top hockey-playing countries in the world. The tournament divided the countries into two divisions: a North American pool and a European pool. The North American pool featured Canada, the United States, Russia and Slovakia. All the games were played in Canada and the United States. The European pool, comprising Sweden, Finland, Germany, and the Czech Republic, contested their preliminary matchups in Stockholm, Sweden; Helsinki, Finland; Garmisch, Germany; and Prague, in the Czech Republic. The playoff rounds would all be played in North America, with the final game to be played in Montreal.

While the tournament did have some exciting moments, it lacked the tension and nerve-wracking anticipation of the early Canada Cup showdowns. Following the fall of the Iron Curtain and the overwhelming arrival in North America of Czech and Russian players, the uniqueness of previous international events such as the Canada Cup and the friendship exhibition tours simply no longer existed.

The final did provide some real excitement, as the USA avenged their loss to Canada in the 1991 Canada Cup by upsetting the home team in the finale of the tournament to capture the first World Cup championship. Mike Richter was named the tournament MVP, overcoming a shaky performance in Game One of the finals to stone the Canadians in the final two matches and give the USA their first major triumph over their northern allies.

BELOW: *Team USA gathers after downing Team Canada in the first World Cup tournament in September 1996.*

RIGHT: *Team USA rearguard Kevin Hatcher catches the elusive Wayne Gretzky during the World Cup finals in 1996.*

The 1996 World Cup

ROUND ROBIN TOURNAMENT RESULTS	
August 26	Sweden 6, Germany 1 (Stockholm)
August 27	Finland 7, Czech Rep 3 (Helsinki)
August 28	Finland 8, Germany 3 (Helsinki)
August 29	Sweden 3, Czech Rep 0 (Prague)
	Canada 5, Russia 3 (Vancouver)
August 31	Germany 7, Czech Rep 1 (Garmisch)
	Russia 7, Slovakia 4 (Montreal)
	United States 5, Canada 3 (Philadelphia)
September 1	Sweden 5, Finland 2 (Stockholm)
	Canada 3, Slovakia 2 (Ottawa)
September 2	USA 5, Russia 2 (New York)
September 3	USA 9, Slovakia 3 (New York)

PLAYOFFS	
September 5	Canada 4, Germany 1 (Montreal)
September 6	Russia 5, Finland 0 (Ottawa)
September 7	Canada 3, Sweden 2, 2 OT (Philadelphia)
September 8	United States 5, Russia 2 (Ottawa)

FINALS	
September 10	Canada 4, USA 3, OT (Philadelphia)
September 12	USA 5, Canada 2 (Montreal)
September 14	USA 5, Canada 2 (Montreal)

The Dominator

There was a definitive shift in focus when the NHL reconvened to open the 1996/97 season. The freewheeling, all-out offensive onslaught that characterized the1980s was replaced by a conservative 'defense-first' policy. Part of the reason for this shift in strategy was the emergence of a new breed of goaltender. These new crease cops were agile, acrobatic and athletic. They also were equipped with lighter, more flexible and larger-than-life pads, blockers and trappers.

The ace of the goaltending fraternity was a slight goaltender, with a spine like a Slinky toy, from the Czech Republic who quickly earned the nickname 'The Dominator.' Dominik Hasek, who often appeared to be a human pretzel on skates, became the first goaltender since the Ken Dryden-Bernie Parent-Tony Esposito era to truly control the entire focus of the game. Hasek's outstanding work between the pipes helped lead the Sabres to a top-spot finish in the Northeast Division with a goaltending style that defied description. Whether it was using his blocker to snag loose pucks, laying his goal stick along the goal line to halt rolling pucks or tossing his fragile frame across the crease to nab a hot shot, Hasek was willing, able and capable of doing it. In the 1996/97 season, he recorded a goals-

BELOW AND RIGHT: *Teemu Selanne (below) and Paul Kariya (right) combined to give the Anaheim Mighty Ducks the NHL's top 1-2 offensive punch during their six seasons together.*

FAR RIGHT: *Dominik 'The Dominator' Hasek flashes the style that helped him capture a pair of MVP awards in 1996/97 and 1997/98.*

ABOVE: *Detroit's Brendan Shanahan (14) closes ranks on Philadelphia's Dainius Zubrus during Detroit's four-game sweep of the Flyers in the 1997 Finals.*

RIGHT: *Darren McCarty, seen here upending Washington's Richard Zednik during the 1998 Stanley Cup Finals, has developed into one of the NHL's top two-way forwards.*

against average of 2.27, racked up 37 wins and became the first goaltender since Jacques Plante to win the Hart Trophy as the NHL's most valuable player.

While Hasek was establishing himself as the feel-good story of the year, a sadder script was being written in Pittsburgh. Mario Lemieux – the most explosive offensive weapon to skate in the NHL since Rocket Richard and Mike Bossy – announced that he was retiring following the season. Lemieux, who compiled a league-best 72 assists and 122 points, became the first player to retire as the league's defending scoring leader.

The NY Rangers made headlines when they signed Wayne Gretzky to a free agent contract, but even the Great One couldn't help the ragged Rangers light up the Great White Way. Despite a 97-point contribution from Gretzky and a Norris Trophy-winning season from blueliner Brian Leetch, the Broadway Blues finished a disappointing fourth in their division.

In the West, the tandem of Teemu Selanne and Paul Kariya were exciting fans in Anaheim with their inspired play. Selanne returned to his Finnish Flash form, ripping 51 shots past NHL goaltenders. Kariya, whose deft touch and soft hands made him a crowd favorite, proved to be a perfect partner for Selanne. The deadly duo helped the Mighty Ducks reach the playoffs for the first time in team history. After squeezing past Phoenix in a seven-game barn-burner, the Ducks were doused by Detroit in four straight games, although the Wings needed three overtime victories to pluck the Ducks.

Dominik Hasek may have been the outstanding individual story of the season, but it was the play of the Philadelphia Flyers and the Detroit Red Wings that made the bestseller's list. The Flyers had a lethal combination of size, strength and stamina – as exemplified by the hulking presence of Eric Lindros and John LeClair. The Philly phenoms sliced past the Sabres and romped over the NY Rangers to reach the finals for the first time since 1987. Their space in the spotlight was shared by the Detroit Red Wings, who eliminated years of promise and decades of broken dreams by returning to the Stanley Cup penthouse for the first time since 1955. Two key acquisitions helped the Red Wings crush the curse: Aggressive two-way forward Brendan Shanahan and veteran defenseman Larry Murphy provided leadership on and off the ice.

Perhaps the key to Detroit's success lay in a carefully constructed game plan formulated by Scotty Bowman that utilized a defensive system known as the left-wing lock. A variation of the New Jersey Devils' neutral zone trap, the 'lock' cut off passing lanes and slowed down the pace of the opponent's attack. This constant pressure caused turnovers and allowed the Wings to create offense from defense. Against the strong but sluggish Flyers, the Detroit defenders completely shut down the Philadelphia attack, allowing the Red Wings to sweep the series in four efficient, regimented games.

Goaltender Mike Vernon, who tied an NHL record with 16 victories and recorded a miniscule 1.76 goals-against average, was selected as the playoff MVP.

As part of the promotional plan to bring the game into a wider focus, the NHL opened the 1997/98 season with a pair of games in Tokyo, Japan, between the Vancouver Canucks and the Anaheim Mighty Ducks. It marked the first time in league history that regular season games were played outside of North America.

Coincidentally, at the same time, the balance of star power in the NHL was shifting in favor of European-trained players. The top three scorers in the league during the 1997/98 season were products of the European system. Jaromir Jagr was the league's top marksman, collecting 102 points. Finland's Teemu Selanne, Russia's Pavel Bure and the Czech Republic's Peter Bondra all reached the 50-goal plateau.

But once again Buffalo's elastic acrobat, goaltender Dominik Hasek, was the story of the season. Hasek recorded 13 shutouts, the most by any goaltender since Tony Esposito's 15 zeroes in the 1969/70 season. Although the Sabres' express was derailed by the surprising Washington Capitals in the playoffs, Hasek became the only goaltender to win back-to-back Hart Trophy awards as the league's MVP. Hasek's disappointment at missing out on a Stanley Cup parade was compensated for by his outstanding play during the 1998 Olympics as he stonewalled the opposition to lead the underdog Czech Republic team to a gold medal victory.

New Jersey's Martin Brodeur also enjoyed a marvelous season, becoming the first netminder since Bernie Parent to record at least ten shutouts in consecutive seasons. His miniscule goals-against average of 1.89 was also the lowest in the land.

The Washington Capitals were the NHL's most surprising team in the 1997/98 campaign, using inspired leadership from captain Dale Hunter, the potent offense of Peter Bondra and outstanding goaltending from Olaf 'Godzilla' Kolzig to reach the finals. Their opponents were the defending Stanley Cup champion Detroit Red Wings. The Wings used an off-season automobile accident that paralyzed blueliner Vladislav Konstantinov as extra inspiration in their quest to keep the Cup in the Motor City.

The Capitals lacked the polish and experience of the Red Wings, but they managed to give Detroit a solid challenge. After the Wings escaped with a 2-1 win in the series opener, they staged a historic comeback to ward off defeat in Game Two. The Wings became the first team in 42 years to overcome a two-goal deficit in the third period of the championship finals, battling back to record a 5-4 win. The deflating loss weakened Washington's resolve and they meekly succumbed in four straight games.

The Pros Go To Nagano: The 1998 Winter Olympics

As they prepared for the 1997/98 season, the NHL took a brave and bold leap into the future. After months of negotiation, the league, the NHL Players Association and the International Olympic Committee agreed to allow NHL players to compete in the Winter Olympics in Nagano, Japan. As a result, the NHL schedule was tightened and the league agreed to take a ten-day break so the best players in the world could represent their country at the Olympic games.

Despite high hopes, the first ever fully professional Olympic ice hockey tournament was a disappointment. While the on-ice action was at times stimulating, the long-distance travel, lack of preparation time and unfamiliarity with the nuances of the Olympic journey left many of the players confused and tired.

In the end, neither Canada nor the USA was a factor in the medal round. Canada suffered a bitter 2-1 defeat in a shootout against the Czech Republic. The nationalistic tongues of the world's top hockey nation were wagging in disgust after Wayne Gretzky, the game's greatest player, was left off the list in the decisive tie-breaking shootout. The Czech Republic, led by the stingy, spectacular goaltending of Dominik Hasek, captured the gold medal.

The End of an Era

As the 1998/99 season began, there were rumblings out of Rangerland that Wayne Gretzky was preparing to suit up for his final NHL campaign. For his part, the Great One remained stoically silent, but there was no doubt he was extremely disappointed over the Olympic loss and the failure of his Rangers team to make any improvement in the standings.

The other major focus was the addition of another expansion franchise. Hockey married hokum and the Grand Ole Opry as the Nashville Predators made their NHL debut, although they rarely sang in perfect harmony during their freshman season.

After two seasons of turmoil, the Toronto Maple Leafs made headlines by moving into the Eastern Division. While the change of conferences did cut down on travel time and re-establish the grand old Montreal Canadiens/Toronto Maple Leafs rivalry, it also presented the Leafs with a tough task. The East was a hard-as-nails conference where a .500 record was mandatory for making the post-season, a mark the Leafs had not approached since Doug Gilmour was performing his magic on the old Maple Leaf Gardens stage. The Leafs went a long way towards solving that dilemma by signing free agent goaltender Curtis Joseph and super sniper Steve 'Stumpy' Thomas. Joseph, who was renowned for his

RIGHT: *Mats Sundin has led the Toronto Maple Leafs in scoring in each of his eight seasons with the club.*

BELOW: *Top Dog: Toronto's Curtis 'Cujo' Joseph makes another scintillating stop.*

ABOVE: *Mark Messier left the bright lights of Broadway to sign a lucrative free agent contract with the lowly Vancouver Canucks.*

ability to make the big save at the right time, would give the Leafs a solid presence in goal while Thomas, who was best known for his ability to score huge goals in the playoffs, would be the perfect partner for the Leafs captain and main offensive threat, Mats Sundin.

The Leafs may have improved their lineup, but most pundits felt the balance of power in the East rested in the stop 'em and drop 'em brilliance of Buffalo's Dominik Hasek, the bore 'em and snore 'em defensive system of the New Jersey Devils, the bump 'em and bang 'em antics of the Philadelphia Flyers and the run 'em and gun 'em offensive artistry of Alexei Yashin and the improving Ottawa Senators.

In the Western Division, the Dallas Stars moved into a new home and were determined to bring Lord Stanley to Texas. Despite winning the President's Trophy as the top team in the NHL the previous season, the club failed to advance to the Stanley Cup finals. Still, the Stars' brass believed the club needed only fine-tuning, not a major overhaul. Therefore, the team was frugal in its off-season dealings, signing free agent super-sniper Brett Hull and adding face-off specialist Tony Hrkac to their already solid lineup. Colorado introduced two of the league's most-touted rookies in Chris Drury and Milan Hejduk, and both would play key roles in the Avalanche's season. Drury would prove that general manag-

er Pierre Lacroix had a magic touch by capturing rookie-of-the-year accolades after snapping home 20 goals and adding 24 assists. Detroit remained almost steadfast, adding only 1995 Stanley Cup hero Uwe Krupp.

The major stories of the regular season were the offensive wizardry of the Toronto Maple Leafs, the trade of Pavel Bure to Florida and Theo Fleury to Colorado, the steady, focused vision of the Dallas Stars and the continued brilliance of Buffalo's Dominik Hasek.

In Toronto, newly appointed coach and general manager Pat Quinn implemented a furious offensive system that focused on swift puck movement, innovative breakout passing, dazzling speed and good old-fashioned offense. The Leafs led the NHL in goals for the first time since Conn Smythe was a colonel and set team records for wins (45) and road victories (22). Newcomers like Sergei Berezin, Steve Sullivan and Mike Johnson added much-needed youth and vitality, while Steve Thomas (28 goals), Mats Sundin (31 goals) and late-season acquisition Yanic Perreault provided veteran leadership.

Two superstars made bold and brave moves during the season by demanding to be traded to contending franchises. Ironically, while both received their wishes, neither would be able to sustain their previous brilliance or attain on-ice satisfaction in their new homes.

After he refused to report to Vancouver, the Canucks kept Pavel Bure on ice – or rather, off the ice – until 17 January before finally succumbing and dispatching the disgruntled superstar to Florida for Dave Gagner, goaltender Kevin Weekes and rumbling defenseman Ed Jovanovski. A similar situation also arose in Calgary, where the franchise's all-time

leading scorer and potential unrestricted free agent, Theoren Fleury, also sought a move to a more competitive club. At the trade deadline, the Flames traded Fleury to Colorado, the first of a number of clever transactions that Avalanche general manager Pierre Lacroix would pull out of his magician's hat in the upcoming years.

One of the more interesting transformations occurred in Dallas where Brett Hull, long labeled as a one-dimensional albeit brilliant player, became an effective defensive presence while continuing to be a spark plug on offense. Hull's dedication to coach Ken Hitchcock's strict system buoyed the entire club as Dallas climbed to the top of the NHL standings and captured their second consecutive President's Trophy as the NHL's top team. This year, there would be gold at the end of the Stanley Cup reign-bow.

Pittsburgh's Jaromir Jagr won his third consecutive scoring title with 127 points and captured his first Pearson Award as the NHL's top player, as well as his first Hart Trophy as league MVP. In so doing, he broke Dominik Hasek's two-year hold on both prizes. Hasek wasn't shut out on award evening, though, earning a berth on the NHL's First All-Star Team and carting home his third Vezina Trophy as the league's top cage cop. Teemu Selanne led all NHL sharpshooters with 47 goals and took home the Maurice Richard Trophy, while big Al MacInnis, the only defenseman to top the 20-goal plateau, was awarded the Norris Trophy.

Yet, despite some fine individual efforts, the only real story of the 1998/99 season didn't materialize until the final weekend of the schedule. On 18 April 1999, the game's greatest player, all-time leading scorer and most vocally enthusiastic ambassador stepped away from the sport that defined his life and his times. Wayne Gretzky announced his retirement and played his final NHL game, earning an assist on the Rangers' lone goal in a 2-1 loss to Pittsburgh. When the Great One hung 'em up, he held or shared 61 NHL records, including 894 goals and 2857 regular-season points. While he was not the Gretzky of old, he still led the Rangers in points and assists.

The post-season belonged to the Dallas Stars, though they took a bumpy route to reach the winner's circle. The Stars downed the Edmonton Oilers in four straight games in their opening series, with all four games decided by a single tally. The super Stars needed six games (including two overtime wins) to eliminate St Louis and depended on the out-of-this-world antics of goaltender Eddie the Eagle Belfour to take it to the limit against Colorado before surviving another Avalanche to reach the finals for the third time in franchise history.

While the Stars' appearance in the Championship final was hardly a surprise, their opponent in Lord Stanley's dance was a mild shocker. The Buffalo Sabres were thought to be a one-dimensional team, wholly dependent on the goaltending of the Dominator, Dominik Hasek. But coach Lindy Ruff forged the Sabres into a complete team-oriented unit, combining pugnacious fore checking led by team captain Mike Peca with a diligent, patient attack. With Hasek-like efficiency, the Sabres cut a swath through the Eastern Conference, sweeping Ottawa, punching out Boston in six rounds and frustrating Toronto to enter the finals for the second time.

After three successive Stanley Cup final sweeps, NHL fans were finally treated to a competitive Championship series. Unfortunately, the outcome was muddied by one of the league's most questioned and controversial rules. During the opening round of the 1994 playoffs, St Louis goalie Grant Fuhr sustained a season-ending knee injury when he was run over by a rambunctious Toronto Maple Leaf forward. Since that time, the league incorporated a strict in-the-crease rule that stated no part of a player – including skate blades, sticks or even jerseys – could enter the blue ice surrounding the goal area. The no-nonsense rule led to numerous problems, with even empty net goals being disallowed because a player's skate was in the crease, even though there was no goalie to protect at the time. The rule was to be tested to its extreme in the 1999 finals.

Both Buffalo and Dallas played similar games, although with veteran names like Mike Modano, Brett Hull, Joe Nieuwendyk, Mike Keane, Pat Verbeek, Guy Carbonneau, Craig Ludwig, Dave Reid and Derian Hatcher dotting their lineup card, the Stars were clearly winners on paper. Aside from Hasek and Peca, the Buffalo team were muckers like Rob Ray, youngsters like Erik Rasmussen and up-and-coming talent like Miroslav Satan, Alexei Zhitnik and Jason Woolley.

All the games were competitive and closely contested. After five matches, the Stars held a three-games-to-two advantage. Game Six went into triple overtime before Brett Hull swept a rebound past a sprawled Dominik Hasek at the 54:51 mark of extra time to cart the Cup to Texas. The problem was that Hull's skate was skirting the edge of the crease. While he clearly did not interfere with Hasek, the letter of the law stated the goal should have been disallowed. But as soon as the puck crossed the line, the cameras were on the

ice, the Dallas players were scrumming and celebrating and the NHL was powerless to reverse the call. It was a disappointing end to a marvelous season, but the Stars were commended for the victory. Joe Nieuwendyk, who tied a playoff record with six game-winning goals, took home the post-season MVP award, although Ed Belfour's 16 wins and stingy 1.63 GAA warranted consideration.

BELOW: *Unorthodox, enigmatic, and brilliant are some of the adjectives used to describe Buffalo's Dominik Hasek.*

ABOVE: *Often criticized for his lack of defensive motivation, Brett Hull became a valuable two-way player under the guidance of Dallas coach Ken Hitchcock.*

RIGHT: *Joe Nieuwendyk led all NHL scorers during the 1999 post-season with 11 goals.*

A Brave New World

As the league entered a season without Wayne Gretzky for the first time since 1979/80, another superstar returned to the fold, albeit in a completely different role. In September 1999, Mario Lemieux's bid to purchase the Penguins team was approved and he became the new owner of the Pittsburgh club, ensuring the franchise would survive in the Steel City.

Not surprisingly, one of the first orders of business for the league as the 1999/2000 season approached was to deal with the in-the-crease rule. And they did by dropping it altogether and giving jurisdiction on goaltender interference back to the referees (note the plural). The league also decided to continue implementing its two-referee system, increasing the number of double-zebra games to 25 from 20.

Once again, another unhappy superstar highlighted much of the pre-season chatter. Alexei Yashin, the Ottawa Senators marquee star, refused to report to the team unless his contract was renegotiated. The Senators brass remained resolute and suspended the Russian renegade, forcing him to sit out the entire season.

Defensive play continued to dominate the NHL game, leading many critics to ponder whether bench bosses around the league were coaching to win or coaching not to be fired.

BELOW: *Pavel Bure treated fans in Florida to an awesome display of speed, dexterity and talent when he arrived from Vancouver in January of 1999.*

For the first time since 1967/68 no player was able to reach the century mark in points, and only one marksman, Florida's golden boy Pavel Bure, ascended the 50-goal plateau, leading the league with 58 tallies.

No other headline-grabbing story of the regular season matched Boston's decision to trade Ray Bourque, the most popular player not named Bobby Orr ever to wear a Bruins jersey, to the Colorado Avalanche. But that move, like many other choices made during the 1999/2000 season, proved that surging budgets and stocking teams with superstars was hardly a guarantee for success.

The NY Rangers opened the bank vault to sign Theo Fleury but still managed to miss the playoffs for the fourth consecutive season. The Anaheim Mighty Ducks had the fourth (Paul Kariya, 86 points) and fifth (Teemu Selanne, 85 points) high scorers in the league in their everyday lineup and still finished last in their division. Tony Amonte of Chicago and Valeri Bure of Calgary each reached the 40-goal plateau, but neither of their clubs was able to reach the playoffs.

But there were teams who were able to combine budget, scouting and careful trades to develop a winning franchise, with decidedly different results.

The St Louis Blues finally reached a pinnacle in the team's history. The Blues won the NHL's regular-season crown, buoyed by the NHL's top two-man defensive tandem of Chris Pronger and Al MacInnis, the offensive talents of Pierre Turgeon, top-notch newcomer Pavol Demitra and a rejuvenated Scott Young. The surging Blues collected a team record 114 points and a league-high 51 victories. Unfortunately for the

ABOVE AND RIGHT: *Blessed with size, speed, strength and smarts, St Louis defenders Chris Pronger (above) and Al MacInnis (right) are the leaders along the Blues' blueline. Pronger captured the Hart Trophy as NHL MVP in 1999/2000 while MacInnis was named as the NHL's top rearguard in 1998/99.*

hockey faithful in Missouri, St Louis faced legendary giant killers San Jose in the first round of the playoffs. The Blues got bit by the Sharks in a tough seven-game marathon and had to watch an entire season, the finest in franchise history, end in shockingly decisive fashion.

The real architect of building Stanley Cup calibre teams with a limited budget remained the New Jersey Devils' Lou Lamoriello. A no-nonsense, tough-as-nails negotiator, Big Lou has always been a savvy prognosticator – able to predict how to stay within his budget, able to predict just what it would take to whittle down a player's salary request to a workable equation, discover and sign sprouting talent other teams neglected and always turn a profit. In 1999/2000, Lamoriello laughed all the way to the bank.

Two players who exemplified Lamoriello's ability to find diamonds in the rough were Scott Gomez and Brian Rafalski. Gomez, the first Mexican-American player to play in the NHL, was a free agent from the University of Alaska who went on to win the Rookie of the Year award. Rafalski, another US college veteran who spent the first four years of his pro career in Europe, became one of the Devils' top defensemen, combining clever offensive instincts with determined defense.

Although they could not match the offensive marks they set in the previous season, the Toronto Maple Leafs reached the 100-point mark for the first time in team history. After dumping Ottawa in the opening round, however, the Leafs were unable to withstand the physical punishment dished out by the Devils and surrendered in six games.

Philadelphia, led by rookie Brian Boucher who topped all NHL netminders with a 1.91 GAA, topped the Eastern Conference with 105 points, but they were also unable to withstand the overpowering physical dominance of the Devils in the playoffs. The Flyers/Devils series was more war than fair as both clubs used a brutal, hard-hitting strategy in an attempt to gain the upper hand. After six games, the series was leveled at three games apiece, with Game Seven guaranteeing a spot in the Stanley Cup spotlight.

Perhaps the key to the entire post-season success of the Devils came when Devils captain Scott Stevens leveled Eric Lindros with a devastating hit that knocked the Flyers captain out of the game. That knockout blow seemed to demoralize the Philadelphia players, allowing Jersey to hold on for a 2-1 win. The victory advanced New Jersey to the Championship finals, where they would meet another tough adversary, the defending champion Dallas Stars.

The Dallas Stars had played more high-tension hockey over the previous 16 months than any other team on earth. But after surviving a rough seven-game set with the Colorado Avalanche just to reach the finals, it's safe to surmise the Stars were running on fumes. Finally, the wheels slowed down and the gas ran out, mainly because the fresher New Jersey Devils had a game plan to physically punish the Stars and the strategy eventually paid dividends. But it came at a price.

New Jersey needed a goal by Bill Guerin at the 28:20 mark of overtime in Game Six of the finals before the Stars relinquished their crown. In 2000/01, it would be the Devils who would succumb to the physical torture of trying to repeat as champions.

Scott Stevens, who provided a dominating physical presence that both intimidated and inspired, won the Conn Smythe Trophy as playoff MVP.

LEFT: *Scott Stevens is the 'Minister of Defense' for the New Jersey Devils, delivering bone-crunching hits on any member of the opposition who strays into his office.*

Avalanche!

The 2000/01 season saw two of hockey's greatest post-expansion superstars making surprise comebacks, one in the boardroom and one on the ice. In addition, one reluctant star returned to the NHL fold while two other star players endured contractual freezes with their parent clubs that would tarnish the entire campaign.

After months of negotiation, Wayne Gretzky announced he was returning to the game as a part owner of the Phoenix Coyotes. Since that rumor had been circulating for months, it was greeted with only limited acclaim. Although the negotiations to confirm the transaction were often arduous and time-consuming, the deal was sealed on 15 February 2001 and Wayne Gretzky and partner Steve Ellman officially took over the reins of the Arizona franchise.

Even the most tuned-in media members were taken by surprise when, on 11 December 2000, Mario Lemieux announced he was returning to the Pittsburgh Penguins as an active player. Most scribes denounced Number 66's return as propaganda to promote the sagging fortunes of his Penguins franchise, but they obviously misunderstood the drive and desire of this incredible athlete. On 27 December, Lemieux made a spectacular return to the ice, collecting an assist only 34 seconds into the Penguins' game against the

BELOW: *Mario Lemieux became the first Hall of Fame member since Guy Lafleur to play in the NHL when he rejoined the Pittsburgh Penguins midway through the 2000/01 season.*

Toronto Maple Leafs. The Magnificent One accumulated 76 points in just 43 games that season and helped lead the Penguins to the Eastern Conference Finals.

In Ottawa, Alexei Yashin's lawsuit to have his contract voided was overturned, forcing the reluctant superstar to return to the Capital City club. In Buffalo, Mike Peca and the Sabres failed to come to terms on a new deal, while the Philadelphia story was the soap opera love/hate affair between Eric Lindros and Philly general manager Bob Clarke, which provided the media with a plethora of accusations, rumors, angry banter and great copy.

As the Colorado Avalanche prepared for the 2000/01 season, veteran Ray Bourque called a team meeting. A shy, soft-spoken individual, Bourque led by example, not by words. Still, he felt compelled to say a few words to the teammates he barely got to know the previous season. Bourque wanted to instill a sense of desperation among the troops, and motivate them toward only one purpose and one goal: to win the Stanley Cup.

Mr Bourque did not have to be eloquent or adamant in his speech. He not only had the respect of the entire Avalanche dressing room, he also was revered by the whole hockey world. There wasn't a fan alive with a real passion for the sport that wasn't pulling for the five-time Norris Trophy recipient, the 18-time NHL All-Star and the 21-year veteran to finally get the opportunity to raise the Stanley Cup above his head. To help ensure that Bourque's dream would reach fruition, general manager Lacroix managed to acquire Rob Blake, the best defenseman in the league not

named Lidstrom or MacInnis, from the LA Kings in a brazen pre-trade deadline coup.

In 2000/01, the NY Rangers were able to pry general manager Glen Sather and coach Ron Lowe from the cash-challenged Edmonton Oilers. Still, the Oilers, with Kevin Lowe at the helm and Craig McTavish behind the bench, finished with 20 more points than the Broadway Blues. Edmonton made the playoffs and forced the Dallas Stars to win three overtime games before falling in a six-game marathon that provided hockey fans with the best action of the entire playoffs.

Jaromir Jagr won his fifth straight scoring title with 121 points and Pavel Bure led the league in goals with 59. Nic Lidstrom was named the NHL's top rearguard, while New Jersey's Patrick Elias, Boston's Jason Allison and Pittsburgh's Alexei Kovalev all established themselves as the new elite of the NHL.

For the rest of the league that season, it was 'read 'em and weep', because nothing seemed to make perfect sense.

ABOVE: *The Detroit Red Wings' Nicklas Lidstrom was named* *the NHL's top defenseman in 2000/01.*

• Alexei Yashin returned to the Ottawa Senators and led the club in scoring but was painfully dormant as the Sens fell in the playoffs in four straight games to the Toronto Maple Leafs.

• Mark Messier returned to the NY Rangers but the Rangers missed the playoffs again.

• Dominik Hasek threatened to retire, came back and then got injured. His absence cancelled any and all of Buffalo's post-season hopes.

• The Detroit Red Wings, who tied for the NHL lead with 111 points in the regular season, lost to the LA Kings in the opening round of the playoffs. The key to the Kings' victory was a remarkable comeback in Game Four when the Wings blew a

two-goal lead with less than two minutes remaining and lost in overtime. That loss deflated Detroit and they bowed out of the post-season in six games.

• The St Louis Blues avenged their playoff loss to San Jose in 2000, swept the Dallas Stars in round two but lost two overtime games in a row against Colorado and were denied a trip to the Championship round.

• Four members of the top ten in scoring in 2000/01 would be with different clubs in 2001/02, two others would miss all or most of the 2001/02 season and only one, Joe Sakic, would keep his place among the NHL's top ten scorers in 2001/02.

All eyes were focused on Colorado during the regular season, where the Avalanche and Ray Bourque had a magical campaign. Led by Hart Trophy recipient Joe Sakic, Colorado breezed to the top of the NHL regular-season ladder with 118 points. Both Sakic (118 points) and Peter Forsberg (89 points) finished among the top ten scorers, Patrick Roy became the NHL's winningest goaltender, surpassing the immortal Terry Sawchuk, and Ray Bourque was selected to the NHL's First All-Star Team for the thirteenth time.

In the playoffs, the Avalanche survived a second-round

ABOVE: Ray Bourque, whose Number 77 has been retired by both Boston and Colorado, finally had his name engraved on the Stanley Cup as a member of the Avalanche in 2001.

scare against the upstart LA Kings to ditch St Louis in five games and motor into the Championship round. Their opponents were the defending champion New Jersey Devils who, like the Dallas Stars before them, could not overcome the physical and emotional strain of trying to repeat as champions. They gave an excellent account of themselves, bouncing back from a 3-1 deficit to even the series at three apiece, sending the Championship round to a seventh game for the first time since 1994 and only the second time since 1987. The Avalanche rolled to a convincing 5-1 victory in Game Seven, bringing Lord Stanley to the mountains and lifting a mountain off the shoulders of Ray Bourque. The all-time leading scorer among defenseman in NHL history could now retire as a champion.

Seconds after accepting the Stanley Cup from Commissioner Gary Bettman, Conn Smythe Trophy recipient Joe Sakic immediately offered the silverware to Bourque, who raised the Cup high above his head in a salute the entire hockey world appreciated.

ABOVE: *Joe Sakic, who lets his outstanding play on the ice do the talking for him, is one of only four team captains to win the MVP award and the Stanley Cup in the same season.*

RIGHT: *Rob Blake (4) solidified the Avalanche blueline when he was obtained from the LA Kings in February 2001.*

OVERLEAF: *Dominik Hasek displays his sprawling style in goal for the Buffalo Sabers.*

Onward and Upward

When Wayne Gretzky made his NHL debut in October 1979, the popularity of ice hockey in the United States was in serious decline. By the end of the 1970s the Eastern Hockey League, Southern Hockey League, North American Hockey League, Pacific Hockey League and the World Hockey Association had all folded. The USHL, the pre-eminent senior/amateur league in the country which had been as competitive as any major pro circuit, had transformed itself into a junior league, featuring players under the age of 21.Three of the WHA franchises absorbed by the NHL were based in Canada, and there was serious concern for the health of the sport south of the Canadian border. Many pro players who were not candidates for NHL contracts went to Europe to continue their careers since there simply were not enough teams in North America.

By the time the Great One was considering hanging up his blades, hockey had made a remarkable recovery in the United States. Team USA's 'Miracle on Ice' gold medal victory in the 1980 Winter Olympics, the emergence of the NY Islanders as a dynasty team, a general crackdown in the 'goon' tactics employed by the Philadelphia Flyers in the 1970s and the eventual trade of Gretzky to the LA Kings all converged to give the game a wider profile in the States. By 1997/98, there were seven professional leagues – not including the NHL – operating in the United States, with 111 different teams dotting the ice hockey map throughout the

country. Interestingly, there were more professional teams in Texas than there were in all of Canada.

Since Gretzky retired, however, there has been a noticeable dip in the sport's allure. Without its marquee star and most vocal advocate, the sport has lost much of its voice. When the 2001/02 season began, the IHL, one of the longest-operating leagues in history, had closed its doors, though some teams were admitted to the AHL. The Western Professional Hockey League also folded, with the Central Hockey League adding a few stray franchises from that league. It was the first time since the 1970s that two major pro leagues folded in the same year.

While Canada had suffered an alarming loss of both prestige and domination in recent years, the 2001/02 season brought Canada and Canadian-born talent to the forefront once again. Both the men's and women's Olympic teams won gold medals at the Salt Lake City games, and for the first time in a decade the statistical leader board was dominated by Canadian players, with six of the top ten scorers calling the Great White North home.

In the United States, a number of 'feel good' stories carried the 2001/02 campaign. The Boston Bruins, with a carefully structured lineup of role players and cagey veterans, climbed to the top of the Eastern Division standings after missing the playoffs in the previous two seasons. The Chicago Blackhawks, a team that had always prided itself on consistency, had failed to earn an invitation to the post-season dance in four straight years. In 2001/02, with super-motivator and tough taskmaster Brian Sutter behind the bench, the Hawks collected over 90 points for the first time in six seasons and easily waltzed into the post-season. The NY

BELOW: *Saku Koivu (11) won the hearts of sports fans when he battled cancer in 2001/02.*

RIGHT: *The Calgary Flames' Jarome Iginla was the NHL's leading goal-scorer in 2001/02.*

undergone an embarrassing evolution. The club fired coaches, appointed new general managers and even were sold to an American businessman. A plethora of injuries, many of the season-ending variety – including a life-threatening throat injury to Trent McCleary that ended his career – had besieged the team. The Habs failed to advance to the playoffs in three straight years, a dry spell that had not occurred since the earliest days of the NHL's existence.

Only days before the Canadiens were sent to training camp, team captain Saku Koivu was diagnosed with non-Hodgkin's lymphoma. The Canadiens used that illness as a springboard to put aside all the sickbay troubles the team had been forced to endure, and the club played inspired, consistent and entertaining hockey all season long.

Remarkably, not only did Koivu recover from the potentially lethal disease, he also had a triumphant comeback on 9 April in a game against the Ottawa Senators. The Habs won the game 4-3, and by doing so secured themselves a treasured spot in the playoffs.

Islanders, who had acquired Alexei Yashin, Mike Peca and Chris Osgood during the off-season, improved their record by over 40 points and made the playoffs for the first time in eight years.

In Calgary, an emerging superstar was gathering most of the accolades. Jarome Iginla, a Canadian-born and -trained player, was the surprise story of the season. Iginla, who had never collected more than 71 points in a single season, became the first North American player to win the Maurice Richard Trophy as the NHL's leading goal-getter and also was the first player not named Jagr to win the scoring title since 1997. History of a different kind was also made in Alberta, as both the Flames and the Edmonton Oilers missed the playoffs for the first time since either team entered the league.

The play of the Detroit Red Wings received much of the sportswriters' ink over the course of the 2001/02 campaign. The bitter sense of loss the Wings experienced in their opening round loss to the LA Kings in 2001 made the club brass even more adamant to make whatever moves necessary to bring the Cup back to Detroit. The Wings added offensive punch in signing both Brett Hull and Luc Robitaille, goaltending savvy in Dominik Hasek, and blueline depth in Jiri Slegr and Fredrik Olausson. As a result, the Wings ran away with the regular-season crown, finishing almost 20 points ahead of their nearest competitors. The Wings also became the first team in NHL history to have four 500-goal scorers (Hull, Steve Yzerman, Brendan Shanahan and Robitaille) on their active roster.

The Dallas Stars, who had been Stanley Cup finalists in 2000, went through a difficult transitional season. General manager Bob Gainey resigned early in the season and coach Ken Hitchcock was fired shortly before the Olympic break. The Stars missed the playoffs for the first time since the 1992/93 season.

But the emotional and inspirational highlight of the season came on a Tuesday night in April at the Molson Centre in Montreal. Over the previous three years, the Canadiens, once the proudest franchise in all of professional sports, had

The 2002 Winter Olympics

The 2002 Olympic ice hockey tournament promised to be an even more competitive affair than the 1998 series. Many of the top European teams, including the gold-medal-winning Czech Republic team, had had numerous 'club' players on their rosters, as in non-NHLers. With a full four years to prepare, the top six countries had stocked their lineups with top NHL talent.

After the bitter disappointment of not participating in the sudden-death shootout at the 1998 Games and the failure to capture a medal, Wayne Gretzky was given a chance at redemption when he was named general manager for Canada's entry at the 2002 Games. Gretzky assembled a team ripe with potential Hall of Fame members. Veterans Steve Yzerman, Joe Sakic, Al MacInnis and Chris Pronger joined young stars such as Simon Gagne and Jarome Iginla to give the Canadian squad a powerhouse lineup.

The USA looked into the past and recruited Herb Brooks to coach their club, hoping for another 'Miracle on Ice' redoux. Featuring luminaries such as Mike Modano, Chris Chelios and John LeClair, the USA team was favored to make it all the way to the gold medal game.

The tournament itself exhibited some of the most exciting, fast-paced hockey seen in some time. Every game was competitive, clean and quickly played.

After rolling through the preliminary round, Team Sweden was eliminated by Belarus in a shocking upset. Canada started slowly, losing to Sweden and squeezing by Germany before rolling on to the gold medal game.

The USA played consistent, high-energy hockey, knocking off every opponent as they rollicked into the dream final – Canada versus the USA. Canada, with the bitter taste of the 1996 World Cup defeat still lingering, played a careful, confident game. Physically stronger and more agile on defense, the Canadians nailed every USA player who crossed the blueline. After surrendering an early goal, the Canucks took control of the match, laying on the body at every opportunity.

Joe Sakic, who was named Olympic MVP, connected for a pair of goals as Canada downed their neighbors to the south by a 5-2 score. The win brought the gold medal to Canada for the first time in five decades. Amazingly, the victory came 50 years to the day after the Edmonton Mercurys captured Canada's last ice hockey gold medal. Team USA captured the silver medal while Team Russia captured the bronze.

The 2002 Stanley Cup playoffs was a six-week war of attrition that featured numerous twists and turns, shocks and surprises and finally, affirmations and reflections.

Fans were also treated to a rare display of bravery and courage when Peter Forsberg and Saku Koivu – both of whom missed the entire regular season – made inspirational returns to their respective teams. Forsberg led all post-season scorers with 27 points while Koivu helped guide the Montreal Canadiens into the Eastern Conference semifinals.

In the opening round of the playoffs, the Red Wings rebounded from a pair of opening losses to Vancouver and outscored the Canucks 16-6 over the next four games to escape with a six-game series victory. The Wings then jettisoned St Louis in five matches before staging one of the season's greatest comebacks, against Colorado. Down 3-2 in games, the Wings climbed up and over the Avalanche by blanking the defending champs in back-to-back games to fly into the championship round.

It's doubtful that a single prognosticator would have succeeded in predicting the Red Wings' opponent in the Finals. The two odds-on favorites to reach the finals – Philadelphia and New Jersey – both lost in the opening round. Ottawa and Montreal both collapsed and dropped off the playoff trail in round two, leaving the Toronto Maple Leafs and the upstart

ABOVE LEFT: *Dominik Hasek, who registered a 1.86 GAA in the 2002 playoffs, set a new NHL record by recording six post-season shutouts.*

LEFT: *Though hobbled by a bad knee and in constant pain, Steve Yzerman led the Red Wings in post-season scoring in 2002 with 17 assists and 23 points.*

RIGHT: *The all-time leading scorer in Hurricanes history, Ron Francis helped guide Carolina into the Stanley Cup finals with six goals and 16 points in the 2002 playoffs.*

BELOW: *Arturs Irbe, who recorded 10 victories and a magnificent 1.67 GAA in the 2002 playoffs, ran out of miracles in the finals when Detroit doused the Hurricanes.*

Carolina Hurricanes battling for the right to face Detroit. The 'Canes' solid defensive zone coverage and patient attack frustrated the Leafs and allowed Carolina to down the Leafs in six games, including three 2-1 overtime wins.

Carolina proved to be a formidable adversary for the veteran Wings. The Hurricanes featured a solid mix of youth (Erik Cole, Bates Battaglia), size (Sean Hill, Ed Ward), speed (Sammi Kapanen, Brent Hedican) and savvy (Ron Francis, Rod BrinD'amour). But, in a series against a team stacked with as many as nine future Hall of Fame members, the Hurricanes storm was reduced to a mere drizzle. Bolstered by Dominik Hasek's record-setting six shutouts, the gritty determination of Steve Yzerman and the behind-the-bench genius of Scotty Bowman, Detroit eclipsed the Hurricanes in five games. Yzerman led all Red Wing scorers with 21 points, while Brett Hull slipped a playoff-high 10 pucks behind enemy netminders. Igor Larianov, the oldest player in the NHL, played like a frisky teenager, notching the winning goal in Game Three with only minutes left in the third overtime period. Nic Lidstrom became the first European-trained player to win the playoff MVP award.

But the most touching moment came last. In 1968, Scotty Bowman's mentor, Toe Blake, had announced his retirement after winning his ninth Cup title. After the final whistle, Bowman donned the blades, lifted the grand old Cup and retired after capturing an NHL record tenth championship (nine as a coach, one as an NHL executive). Mr. Bowman will not be going into the Hall of Fame, however: He's already there.

Today's Top Talent

Rob Blake

One of the NHL's top defensemen, Rob Blake combines offensive dexterity with hard-nosed defense. A mobile, graceful skater and a pinpoint passer, Blake was the 'Minister of Defense' for the LA Kings for 12 seasons before being dealt to the Colorado Avalanche prior to the 2001 playoffs. The presence of Blake on the Avalanche blueline gave the club three potential Hall of Fame rearguards. Blake collected 19 points in 23 games as Colorado returned to the Stanley Cup winner's circle for the second time in franchise history.

ABOVE: *Rob Blake, who led all NHL rearguards with six goals in the 2002 playoffs, mixes speed with an uncanny knack for delivering perfect passes.*

RIGHT: *Pavel Bure, who became the only Vancouver Canuck to win the Calder Trophy as the NHL's top freshman in 1992, has reached the 50-goal plateau four times in his career.*

Pavel Bure

Ever since they entered the league in 1970, the Vancouver Canucks had been searching for a superstar. In 1991, he arrived. He was Pavel Bure, the 'Russian Rocket,' and the Pacific Coliseum faithful welcomed their neighbor from the far West. Bure exhibited all the skills of a Russian star; he is disciplined defensively, can skate like the wind, and can find a teammate's stick through a maze of legs for an easy tap in at the crease.

A natural right winger, Bure played every forward position in his rookie season. In 65 games, he scored 34 goals and 60 points, totals which won him the Calder Trophy, but not a membership on the 1991 All-Rookie Team. He was a contender on either wing, and when the votes were counted for the team roster, Bure had more total votes than any player at any one position, but they were spread across the ice, giving him the dubious honor of becoming the first Calder Trophy winner not to be selected to the All-Rookie Team.

After seven seasons in Vancouver, Bure was traded to Florida, where he continued to pump pucks into opposing nets. He led the NHL in goals in both 1999/2000 (58) and 2000/01 (59), winning the Maurice 'Rocket' Richard Trophy in both seasons. Although his production fell off in 2001/02, Bure was revitalized after being traded to the NY Rangers late in the campaign.

Dominik Hasek

Known in NHL arenas as The Dominator, Dominik Hasek was the NHL's top goaltender during the 1990s. The only goaltender in NHL history to win the league's MVP award twice, Hasek was the backbone of the Buffalo Sabres team, leading them to the Stanley Cup finals in the 1999/2000 season. Hasek has led the NHL in shutouts four times, and became the first goaltender since George Hainsworth to record six shutouts in one month, a feat he accomplished in December 1997. Blessed with sharp reflexes, exemplary concentration and extraordinary foot speed, Hasek has a supple spine that allows him to flip and flop to make even ordinary saves seem complex. Prior to the 2001/02 season, Hasek was traded to Detroit, recording the first 40-win season of his career in helping the Red Wings capture the President's Trophy and the Stanley Cup.

BELOW: *Dominik Hasek put the crowning touch on his Hall of Fame career by adding his name to the Stanley Cup with the 2001/02 Detroit Red Wings.*

RIGHT: *Brett Hull led all NHL sharpshooters with 10 goals and two short-handed markers during the 2002 playoffs.*

Brett Hull

Nicknamed 'The Golden Brett,' Brett Hull was the NHL's foremost goal-scorer in the 1990s, reaching the 70-goal plateau three times in the decade. After whipping 72 shots behind opposition goaltenders in 1989/90, Hull established an NHL single-season record for right-wingers by scoring 86 goals in 1990-91. The son of Hall of Famer Bobby Hull, Brett won the Hart Trophy in 1991 as the league's MVP, and represented the St Louis Blues in seven All-Star games.

Signed as a free agent by Dallas in 1998, Hull scored the Stanley Cup-winning goal for the Stars in 1999. He signed with Detroit as a free agent prior to the 2001/02 season and helped lead the Red Wings to a Stanley Cup victory in 2002.

Jarome Iginla

A former first-round draft selection of the Dallas Stars, Jarome Iginla established himself as one of the NHL's dominant new talents in 2001/02, capturing both the Maurice Richard Trophy for scoring the most goals during the season and the Art Ross Trophy as the NHL's top scorer. While Iginla was always considered to be a potential star, his ascent to the top of the league's scoring ladder was unequalled in recent NHL history. It's safe to say there was not a single NHL scribe who predicted that Iginla would win the 2001/02 NHL scoring title. Not since Roy Conacher took home the Art Ross Trophy in 1948/49 has someone come completely out of nowhere to lead the league in points. Iginla was the Sporting News Player of the Year in 2001/02.

LEFT: *Jarome Iginla topped the NHL in goals and points in 2001/02.*

Jaromir Jagr

Jaromir Jagr of the Czech Republic quickly established himself as an NHL superstar. A talented skater and a superb stickhandler with a flair for the dramatic, Jagr is one of the league's most inventive players. Many NHL defensemen have been left out in the cold after being tricked by one of Jagr's dreaded 'inside-out' maneuvers.

A first-round draft selection of the Pittsburgh Penguins in the 1990 entry draft, he was the first Czech player to be able to attend the NHL entry draft without having to defect. In 1990/91, he made his NHL debut, collecting 27 goals and 30 assists to earn a berth on the NHL's All-Rookie Team. In the playoffs, he played a major role in the Penguins' drive to the Stanley Cup title, contributing 13 points to the cause in 24 postseason games.

In 1998/99, his ninth NHL season, Jagr reached career highs in assists (83) and points (127). In 2000/01, he became only the second player in NHL history to capture four consecutive scoring titles. Jagr was traded to the Washington Capitals prior to the 2001/02 campaign.

BELOW: *Now with the Washington Capitals, Jaromir Jagr remains one of the NHL's premier talents.*

Curtis Joseph

Although he went undrafted and was often considered too slight in size ever to become a serviceable NHL goaltender, Curtis Joseph proved the pundits wrong. Joseph is one of the new breed of NHL goaltenders. He takes a cerebral approach to the game, and often his finest saves are executed because he has researched the opposing shooter and knows that player's tendencies. Combine that with razor-sharp reflexes and a smooth consistent style, and you have the prototype for the modern NHL goalie. Joseph, who patrolled the crease in efficient fashion for both St Louis and Edmonton before joining the Toronto Maple Leafs, has recorded five 30-win seasons in his 13 seasons in the NHL.

Mark Messier

Throughout his illustrious career, Mark Messier has been recognized as one of the game's most respected leaders. After leading the Edmonton Oilers to a surprise Stanley Cup victory in 1990, Messier was traded to the New York Rangers and immediately led the Broadway Blues to the top of the NHL standings for the first time since 1942, and to the Stanley Cup championship in 1994. One of only two players to win the Hart Trophy with two different teams, Messier has appeared in 11 All-Star games and has been selected as post-season All-Star on five separate occasions.

After guiding the Rangers to the Stanley Cup championship in 1994, Messier's career had been remarkably unremarkable. He signed with Vancouver in 1997, but failed to lead the team into the playoffs during his seasons with the club. Messier returned to the NY Rangers in 2000/01.

ABOVE AND LEFT: *Despite injury, Curtis Joseph guided the Leafs into the 2002 playoffs.*

RIGHT: *Back with the NY Rangers, Mark Messier has proven he can still provide spark and smarts.*

Mike Modano

A Michigan boy, Mike Modano was used to cold rinks and bus rides when he arrived in Prince Albert, Saskatchewan, to play for the Raiders. It was only a matter of hard work and patience before Modano was on the minds of general managers around the NHL. In 1988, Minnesota had the trump card at the annual rookie auction, and they took Modano, making him the first American to be selected first overall in the NHL entry draft.

Since then, Modano has become one of the NHL's finest two-way players. In 1992/93, he came into his stride, scoring 93 points to lead the North Stars, and represented the team in the 1993 and 1994 All-Star games. A relentless forechecker and a natural leader, Modano continues to be one the NHL's most effective two-way centers. He has compiled four consecutive 30-goal seasons with the Dallas Stars. A Second Team All-Star in 2000/01, he has represented his country in eight major international tournaments.

Chris Pronger

The emergence of Chris Pronger as one the NHL's top defensemen is a major reason why the St Louis Blues have continued to be perennial playoff contenders. In 2001/02, the Blues made their 23rd consecutive post-season appearance, the finest record among the current NHL clubs by a large margin. The first blueliner to capture both the Hart Trophy and the Norris Trophy in a single season since Bobby Orr, Pronger combines a dominant physical presence with intuitive offensive skills.

LEFT: *The all-time leading scorer in the history of the Stars' franchise, Mike Modano is active in the Make-a-Wish Foundation and United Cerebral Palsy charities.*

ABOVE: *Chris Pronger's presence on the blueline has helped transform the St Louis Blues into an NHL powerhouse and top Cup contender.*

Patrick Roy

When he first burst upon the scene during the 1985/86 season, Patrick Roy was mainly known for his superstitious style of craning his neck like some prehistoric bird and talking to his goalposts. It wasn't long before NHL observers recognized that Roy was one of the finest NHL goaltenders of all time. Roy, the only goaltender to win two or more Stanley Cup titles with two different teams (the Canadiens, in 1985/86 and 1992/93, and the Avalanche, in 1995/96 and 2000/01), became the NHL's all-time winning netminder during the 2000/01 season, surpassing Terry Sawchuk's record of 447 victories.

Patrick Roy was the youngest goaltender to be named as the playoff MVP when he captured the Conn Smythe Trophy in 1986. He is also the only player to win the award with two different teams, grabbing the honor as a member of the Colorado Avalanche in 2000/01. Roy is a five-time All-Star who has represented his team in ten NHL All-Star Games.

LEFT: *Patrick Roy won 11 games in the 2002 playoffs.*

BELOW: *Teemu Selanne is now with the San Jose Sharks.*

Teemu Selanne

Nicknamed 'The Finnish Flash,' this Helsinki native was the first Finnish prospect to be drafted in the first round of the NHL entry draft. The Winnipeg Jets held his card in the 1988 draft, and offered him the sort of contract a good prospect from rural Alberta should expect. Selanne, however, was not just a good prospect – he was the unrivaled superstar in his homeland. He refused all offers from the Jets, preferring to stay in Europe, where he was treated with the respect his talent deserved.

When he finally arrived in the NHL, with a multi-year, multi-million-dollar contract with the Jets, he set new standards for rookies in the NHL. In his first season (1991/92), Selanne established a freshman record for goals, scoring 76 times in 84 games. He became the first rookie since Roy Conacher (1938/39) to lead or tie in NHL goals. He won the Calder Trophy, earned a berth on the First All-Star Team, and appeared in the NHL's mid-season classic, the annual All-Star Game.

Traded to Anaheim midway through the 1995/96 season, Selanne rediscovered his offensive spark. The Finnish Flash led the league in goals in both 1997/98 and 1998/99. He was traded to San Jose in 2000/01.